Shropshire STAR

SHROPSHIRE

Pictures from the Past

Shropshire
STAR
SHROPSHIRE
Pictures from the Past

TOBY NEAL and PHIL GILLAM

breedon **books**
PUBLISHING

First published in Great Britain in 2003 by
The Breedon Books Publishing Company Limited
Breedon House, 3 The Parker Centre,
Derby, DE21 4SZ.

ISBN 1 85983 371 3

Printed and bound by Butler & Tanner,
Frome, Somerset, England.

Jacket printing by Lawrence-Allen Colour Printers,
Weston-super-Mare, Somerset, England.

CONTENTS

Acknowledgements

We acknowledge with gratitude the help of the following contributors: Peter Lea, S.R. Turner, Ray Farlow, Shropshire Records and Research Centre, Cliff Cotton, Frank Chatham, Alf Evans, David Wallace, G.H. Davies, Dawn Rice, Bert Catchpole, Kenneth Plain, Mike Hayward, Joyce Danks, Gwen Edwards, Mary Houlston, Michael Pope/Broseley Local History Group, Mary Brown, Arthur Braithwaite, COD Donnington, Olwyn Smith, Betty Hayes, RAF Shawbury, Major Ervin Miller, Carole Bland-Brook, Ivor Garbett, Freda Gibbs, Joyce Pritchard, Bridgnorth Museum, Greg Hackenberg, David Tench, Vera Evans, Beryl Lewis, Liverpool Post, Elaine Rye, M.E. Vere Robbins, Freda Goucher, David Mitchell.

INTRODUCTION

WELL, here it is.

Having brought you books on Shrewsbury, and Telford, we've now gone the whole hog with *Shropshire: Pictures From The Past.*

These pictures, taken from the archives of Shropshire Newspapers and from the collections of contributors, bring home vividly some of the changes which have taken place in the county within living memory.

Some of those changes are dramatic – demolition, rebuilding, new roads, and so on. But others are so gradual and subtle that you hardly notice them, until you study a photograph taken in years gone by which brings home the full impact.

One old picture can bring back a thousand memories.

Few of the photos in this book were taken with an eye to the future. Yet here we are, now – the future – enjoying all those images from years ago.

It is worth bearing this in mind when taking pictures today and tomorrow. One of the problems with old photos which we come across time and time again is that, unless they are adequately captioned, you are left guessing about when (and often where) they were taken, who is who, and generally what it's all about. And there's no-one alive who can tell you.

So even when it's your closest relatives and friends on the photo, give your pic a caption. It may seem bizarre and unnecessary. But when you take a photograph, you are unwittingly creating a historical record. Will your descendants, in 50, 70, or 100 years' time, be able to recognise anyone?

And you never know. A picture you take now could make it into a book like this one day!

Toby Neal
Telford
Summer 2003

VILLAGE LIFE

SHROPSHIRE'S villages are not what they were. Everybody knows the visible story – the schools, post offices and village shops which have closed, leaving them communities which are no longer self-contained.

New homes, of various degrees of sensitivity to the surroundings, have been built.

The handsome Anglican churches, at the spiritual heart of the communities for centuries, have also seen a decline. Some now have congregations which are in single figures.

Then there are the changes which you can't see, and which photos don't capture. These are the changes in people and attitudes.

It's trends wot's to blame. A steady rise in the proportion of "incomers" has profoundly transformed the villages of Shropshire over the past few decades.

Many of them work away, leaving the village for the town or city in the morning, and coming back home to the country in the evening.

The other side of the coin is that often the newcomers are full of get-up-and-go and are at the heart of village life.

Market forces also have an impact. Youngsters who are born and brought up in the village are, in effect, ethnically cleansed as they reach adulthood. They can't afford to live there, so they move out.

So as you look at the photos on the following pages, bear in mind that they show Shropshire's villages in the twilight years of their "traditional" form. Things will never be the same again.

After a shower, St Andrew's Church at Hope Bowdler, near Church Stretton, stands fresh and clear in the sunshine in this September 1954 view. The church suffered storm damage in January 1998 when a lot of tiles came off the bell tower. The repairs revealed that the battens were failing and as a result the building was given a new roof in the millennium year.

This is the Butter Cross at Alveley, near Bridgnorth, which marks the spot where the farmers' wives used to bring their butter to sell in the 18th century. The lady in this 1962 picture is Janet Harvey, of the Broadway, Stourbridge. The photograph was taken by Harry Cartwright of 20 Glebe Lane, Stourbridge.

Welcome to Corrie, Shropshire-style. Youngsters take a walk past the terraced homes of Coronation Street in the mining village of Highley on January 3, 1967. Imagine what the photographer had to do to get this picture! It was taken because it was feared that Highley Colliery was facing closure, and this was a scene-setter to bring home the impact the loss of the pit would have on the village. Highley Colliery did not shut immediately, and struggled on until January 1969, when it was one of the last Shropshire pits to close.

"Is this one of the oldest post offices in Britain?" So asked the original caption to this image from September 1955. We believe the caption writer was referring not to how long the post office had been established here, but rather to the age of the structure in which the post office just happened to be housed. It was in fact Marshbrook post office picturesquely situated off a main road near Church Stretton. The building is a 400-year-old half-timbered cottage and the fellow with the fork is sub-postmaster G. Phillips in his luxuriant garden.

There has been a longstanding tradition of flying flags from the Arbor Tree at Aston-on-Clun, which is seen here in May 1937. The village is said to be the last community in Britain which continues to celebrate Arbor Day, May 29. If, in this photo, some of the flags seem painted on, it may be because some are. In fact, the only one that looks genuine to us is the Union Flag at the top – a 1930s newspaper artist has been rather enthusiastically at work on this print. The village's celebrations have survived some serious troubles in recent years. The most serious – rather obviously – was when the Arbor Tree, a black poplar estimated to be 250 to 350 years old, fell down in September 1995, causing minor damage to a parked car and blocking Mill Street. It had been leaning for some time and eventually seems to have simply given up the ghost. However, villagers quickly planted a replacement to keep the ancient tradition, and the landmark, alive. More recently the problem has been to find enough people willing to continue to organise the celebrations.

The village of Pontesbury in spring 1967, with St George's Church on the left. Built in 1250 on the site of an old Saxon Minster, it was taken down in 1825 and rebuilt on the foundations. The ancient chancel alone remained intact. In the distance is a rather bare-looking Pontesford Hill, which was used in the filming of the last sequences of the 1949 film of Mary Webb's novel *Gone To Earth*. The book was transparently based on various locations in and around Pontesbury, given disguised names. Mary Webb actually lived in Pontesbury for a time and the area is known as Mary Webb Country. These days Pontesford Hill has a rather different appearance – it is cloaked with trees. Incidentally, the experts tell us that Pontesford is correctly pronounced as three syllables. Some modern Salopians have taken to giving Pontesford Hill a nickname, on account of its appearance from certain directions. They call it Bum Hill.

What a splendid building this is! If you went to school here, you would remember those arched windows and those chimneys for the rest of your life. A church and school were combined into one building at Nantmawr near Oswestry. Built in 1875, this imposing structure had the Nantmawr Congregational Chapel in its top portion while the 38 pupils learned their lessons on the ground floor. The year? 1968.

The newspaper of the day reports: "George Francis, aged 81, has lived for 52 years in peaceful Ruyton-XI-Towns. He lives in the Round House, which many years ago was a toll house." The photograph is from July 1954 and, goodness, doesn't the old gentleman look contented, reading his paper in the brilliant sunshine?

Ruyton-XI-Towns in November 1959. The sandstone cross was put up in 1880 at a cost of £50. According to a modern plaque the cross stands on the site of the lock-up of the ancient manor and borough of Ruyton-of-the-Eleven Towns, consisting of the following townships: Ruyton, Coton, Shotatton, Shelvock, Eardiston, Wykey, West Felton, Haughton, Rednal, Sutton, and Tedsmore. The "hole" in the cross used to house a lantern. Many years ago, this was maintained by the village blacksmith, Edward Lloyd. It was his job to light the lamp at dusk.

It seems strange that only around 60 years ago it was apparently safe to walk down the A49 at Leebotwood. To do so today would be reckless in the extreme. The date of this photograph is guesswork, but we're pretty confident that the car is a Ford Eight. These started appearing on Britain's roads around 1933. On the back of the original print the location is described as "Leebotworth" – an old variation of the Leebotwood name, maybe? The thatched building is the Pound Inn, which dates from around 1500. Originally it used to be a property that held animals on their journey to the markets. They used to walk from Shrewsbury to Church Stretton, Craven Arms, Ludlow and so on and it was a stop-off point.

There was a pound there, like a paddock, where the animals would be left overnight. The herdsmen probably stayed at the pub, hence the name The Pound Inn. Research suggests that it became an inn in 1804. It used to brew its own ale and was originally kept by the Dodd family, and their relatives the Evasons between 1806 and 1916. The Lawley hill in the distance has been entirely painted in by a newspaper artist, presumably because it came out only very faintly on the original print.

The garden is overgrown and there is a dilapidated air about the rambling rectory at Stoke-on-Tern in this September 1945 view. It was, however, still apparently inhabited by the rector. His name was Morris-Jones, and he was both a farmer and a rector, who used to like to go shooting. He may have been the last rector to live there. The rector was moved out to Childs Ercall when Childs Ercall and Stoke-on-Tern were linked as one benefice. The diocese sold the rectory and its condition deteriorated. A huge building, about half of it – we think the part in the foreground – was demolished, making the property more manageable from the maintenance point of view. It is these days a private house.

After 250 years, the St Martins almshouses near Oswestry were being modernised. They were to have all-modern conveniences. Even in the midst of the renovation work being carried out, the quiet power of the old place still makes its presence known. This was December 1964. The almshouses were founded in 1698 by Sir John Trevor of Brynkinalt, Speaker of the House of Commons and Master of the Rolls during the reigns of King William III and Queen Anne.

The photographer who took this photograph in Morville on October 4, 1958, was under the impression that this was the ancient village whipping post. But he seems to have been directed to the wrong spot. Somebody obviously put him or her right as the words "whipping post" have been scribbled out on the back of the original print and replaced with "old signpost." Roped in to take a close look were teenagers Christine Bishop and Patricia Watkins, who lived on a nearby housing estate.

After helping lay the tables for school lunch at the Lyon Hall, Hodnet, Mrs Wilma Owen would put on a white coat, pick up her lollipop, and help nearly 100 children across the busy A53 road in the village. She would then help serve the dinner before putting her coat on again and seeing the children safely back to Hodnet School. This picture was taken on December 14, 1965. Mrs Owen, of The Grove, Hodnet, was a school meals superintendent and as she was already paid by Salop County Council for her lunchtime duties, could not be paid for acting as the crossing warden. So at the time of this photograph parents in the village were calling for a full-time traffic warden on duty first thing in the morning and when the children left for home in the afternoon, as well as lunchtimes.

A dangerous corner near Tong Church – often called the Westminster Abbey of the Midlands – was to disappear when the new A41 bypass, seen here under construction, was completed. The scene is from March 1965. *Picture: Peter Lea.*

Stirchley School was facing an uncertain future back on October 3, 1972, when this photograph was taken. But little did the staff and pupils know that it was destined to become one of the most visited schools in the world. Back then Stirchley still had a post office – albeit scheduled to close that November – and a Norman church, although the church authorities wanted to make it redundant. Just over the horizon the sprawling Brookside housing estate in the new town of Telford was being built and it was not long before Stirchley village would be swallowed up. The school dated from 1861 and catered for 30 local children. It had no hall, no indoor toilets, and school meals had to be taken in the village hall. The headmistress was Mrs Margaret Darlington, of Bartlett Road, Dawley, who was assisted by two staff, one of whom, Mrs Jill Smith, is on this picture. Mrs Darlington had been headmistress for 18 years when the school closed at Christmas 1972. The handsome Victorian building was given a life after death. It was taken down brick by brick and rebuilt at Blists Hill Museum, where it is now visited by tourists from all over the world.

Workmen re-erecting the memorial to Bishop Walsham-How, former rector of Whittington, in the garden of remembrance next to the grounds of Whittington Castle. It is April 1971. The memorial was moved to enable road improvements to be made. Working on the memorial are, from left: Mr J. Richards, Mr H.G. Astbury, and Mr David Owen.

James Pritchard chats to his neighbour Mrs Simmons in front of their home, a 15th-century property in Uppington, back in August 1954. The property, with its elaborate carvings on the timbers, used to have a little shop around the back. There are two houses, No 1 and No 2 Tudor Cottage, and Mr Pritchard lived at No 2 and Mrs Simmons at No 1. Mr Pritchard was the grandfather of Graham Hughes of Wellington who says that his (Graham's) granny Beatrice Pritchard and his aunty, Kitty Davies, née Pritchard, used to run a little shop from the house selling sweets, penny chews, Mars Bars, cigarettes and tobacco for the locals up until the late 1960s. "It was a cupboard in the kitchen really and people used to come to the back door. It was all legal and above board. The oak carving which is on the near side of the picture was replaced some years ago by the workers of Uppington Estate. The one carpenter was my uncle, Tom, who was the son of Beatrice and James. So he worked on the building he had lived in for years and years. They did a rubbing of the original carving on the front, a square block under the window, and traced it out to reproduce it on a new piece of oak. The old piece was rotten." He said that inside the house were timbered beams and quarry tile floors. "There were very uneven floors upstairs, as you can imagine. My mother Phyllis lived there for some years when she was growing up."

Mothers collect their prams at the parish church doorway after a service at Albrighton in January 1965.

Albrighton parish councillors occasionally met in the loft of one of the members to escape the sound of the choir's rehearsals down at their normal meeting place – the Old School in Station Road. The singing could sometimes spoil the councillors' concentration so on such nights they moved into the loft of Councillor Keith Worthington's home in High Street. And not even the electric model railway layout on the right tempted them away from their agenda!

Pretty as a picture… Bouldon.

Choirboys pass through an archway of wands held by members of Baschurch Female Friendly Society on June 23, 1957. For 155 years society members had walked from the church to the institute carrying wands of flowers in what was believed to be the only procession of its kind in the country. The wands were made by the women.

A quiet spot in the village of Astley, four miles north-north-east of Shrewsbury and within earshot of RAF Shawbury. This picture is from 1966.

Youngsters from Edgmond Primary School run the gauntlet on January 30, 1968. Every morning and afternoon the 120 children used the narrow, twisting lane to walk to and from the school. The lack of a proper footpath was worrying the local road safety committee and parents. Although the road had a 30mph speed limit, parents said motorists ignored it. And although there had been no accidents to date, many were going to the trouble of collecting their children from school and were banning them from walking down the lane.

This wonderful half-timbered house at Eaton Constantine is called Baxter's House. Richard Baxter, a non-conformist preacher, went to live there in 1615. An old book in the house tells that the house belonged at that time to Richard Baxter's father. This photograph is from 1954. In 1961 the house was up for sale by auction through a Wellington firm of auctioneers. The place was described as a period Elizabethan farmhouse in 96 acres of agricultural and stock land, eight miles from Shrewsbury and five from Wellington.

Two stuffed polar bears which were kept at the Bull's Head, Hinstock, get a brush-up in 1962. On the left is the licensee, Arthur Worthington, who kept the pub for 37 years, while the boy on the right is Percy Pearce. The bears were kept in the Smoke Room, which is the room on the left of the picture. One of them – the female bear on the right – held a tray. Mr Worthington had originally bought the bears from Broughton Hall, near Chester, and he kept what amounted to a small zoo, with live animals like guinea pigs, monkeys, and foreign birds. Mr Worthington was a colourful character known by the locals as "Whacker". He had a set of drums and also figures around the wall like caricatures of some of the Wolves players, and also a skeleton. He used to play the drums behind the bar, and the figures were wired up with fishing line so that when he pressed the foot pedal they would move. Eventually the council began to crack down on his unusual collection and the bears were sold. Mr Worthington left the pub in 1968 and the pub became a shop. Where are the bears now? There is a rumour that one of them was sold to Fox's Glacier Mints. But the firm in Leicester says it has never had a polar bear standing on its hind legs. So, so much for that theory.

The Kynnersley Arms in Leighton, the village where Gladys Meredith – who became better known as the novelist Mary Webb – was born. In this photo, which is date-stamped December 10, 1946, the pub locals are taking their beer among the straw by the old mill wheel. "The mill is likely to feature in a film of one of Mary Webb's books which is scheduled for production by Paul Soskin, now in Hollywood," said the original caption. Presumably this was Gone To Earth, which was not made until 1949 and, as far as we know, in the event the Kynnersley Arms was not used as a filming location. However, in May 2001 the experts from the Channel 4 Time Team television programme descended on the pub, and uncovered a 17th-century blast furnace which had lain hidden beneath the present-day car park, and they also investigated an old corn mill. Today the dust has settled, but visitors are able to examine the ancient corn mill machinery from the comfort of an armchair. Since the Time Team visit a section of glass floor has been installed, offering views of the massive cog-wheel mechanism in the cellar.

This photograph dates from February 1967. The original caption reads thus: "There is no need for these children of Bourton, near Much Wenlock, to ask passersby the familiar question: 'What's the time, Mister?' Now they can see not only the clock on the parish church, but the whole church itself. It has been made possible because several old yew trees, including one said to be 800 years old, have been cut down. The oldest yew used to stand higher than the church tower, but it was felled because it was rotten and there was the danger of branches falling on to the church in a storm."

All Saints Church at Clive on January 25, 1962. The man walking towards us is Mr Harold Williams, nicknamed Sam, who lived at Clive House Cottage. He worked for a Mr and Mrs Renshaw at Clive House where he was a gardener. He was also people's warden at Clive Church. The woman is Mrs Mary Felton, who lived at The Grove, Grinshill. She is probably on her way to a Mothers' Union meeting in Clive Village Hall, which is just out of the picture. And she is quite likely to be carrying scones in her basket.

Mr Sid Rowe was the last of the village blacksmiths at Ticklerton, Church Stretton. He is seen here at the anvil on his final day at the forge in 1956. The forge became a private house. Picture: S.R.. Turner.

Villagers at Edgmond keeping alive an ancient tradition at St Peter's Church on July 1, 1968. The unbroken tradition of Clipping the Church, which takes its origins from Anglo-Saxon times, involves Edgmond residents holding hands around the outside of the church while the choir and clergy form a procession inside the circle and into the church. Edgmond claims to be the only parish in England to have observed this ancient tradition without a break for over 150 years. And it's important that there are as many people as possible there to complete the circle, because if they don't manage it, folklore says ill-luck will befall the parish for the next 12 months.

Claverley Village Hall was an old Army hut, surplus after World War One and erected around the early 1920s. But as this view from June 1965 shows, its best days were behind it. A "thermometer" stood in the Bull Ring in the village recording the success of fundraising efforts towards building a new village hall. The ultimate aim was to raise £6,000, and at the time this picture was taken the fund stood at £700. Not everybody was in favour. Church caretaker Noel Preece said he did not object to a new hall as such, but there were other things which the village needed first, and there were too many people trying to raise money for too many things. In fact it was not until 1982 that a new hall was erected on the same site in Church Street as the old one, at a cost of around £76,000. The old hall was taken down a fortnight beforehand and by that time things were so bad that you could see daylight through the cracks in the wood. However, it had quite recently had a nice new wooden floor. So villagers ensured this was carefully taken out and relaid in the new hall. It's still there. Historically, the original hut and the land had belonged to Mrs Leigh of Chyknell Hall, a sort of lady of the manor, who gave villagers free use of it and paid the upkeep. She died in about 1948. Her nephew Major Gage inherited Chyknell Hall, and gave the village hall to the village. Later he retired to France.

Few people in Cleobury Mortimer know the history of this sandstone block in High Street, insists the October 1962 newspaper story which accompanied this picture. Even Mrs Edith Harris, who spent 40 years in the town before moving to Bewdley (and who is pictured here), was puzzled. The block is in fact the old market cross where, in the 13th century, Hugh de Mortimer erected his gallows. In 1502, the party carrying the body of the young Prince Arthur rested the coffin on the cross during their journey from Ludlow Castle to Worcester Cathedral.

A speeding mini-van is captured on film as it travels through Cockshutt in the sixties. Cockshutt is four miles south of Ellesmere, incidentally, and boasts an attractive red brick church of 1777 and a handful of timber-framed cottages – details which this van driver may have missed!

The interior decor makes an interesting study in this photograph showing Will Green relaxing in the kitchen of Cleobury North Mill. The picture is datestamped May 17, 1939. It was a corn mill, and he would have been the third generation of Greens to live there, at Mill Farm, and his son George was the fourth, leaving about 1972.

This is Holly Cottage, in the north Shropshire village of Loppington, and it was the home (in May 1961) of Mr and Mrs Samuel Harper. It was photographed as an example of one of the few remaining cruck cottages. In cruck building, the roof supports are made of bent tree trunks erected like the keel of an upside-down boat. Originally, wattle and daub made the walls and the roof would have been thatched.

The village hall at Little Wenlock in May 1963. It was near the site of opencast mining operations and was soon demolished to obtain the materials beneath. However, the mining firm was providing villagers with a new hall, work on which had already started. This was to serve the community for years. Then, at the end of 1998, plans emerged in turn to replace this second village hall. In 2001 a final goodbye party was held before this hall was demolished to make way for a third hall, which opened in July 2002. It had been built at a cost of £314,000.

Will Green looks over the pool at Cleobury North Mill in May 1939. It would not be long before the pool was filled in – it certainly seems to have been filled in by 1956. The oak tree was said to have been very old. The talk was that it had been mentioned in the Domesday Book. It was barely alive at the time this picture was taken.

Okay, okay. So it is one of those obviously posed newspaper pictures of yesteryear, but it nevertheless has a certain charm. It is May 1961 and little boys were still wearing short trousers. The lad nearest the ground is pulling at the Loppington Bull Ring. Legend has it that in olden days "to turn the bull ring over" was a challenge to the best man of the village to a fight. It is of course also linked to the appalling bull baiting that once took place. Even when this barbaric "sport" was eventually outlawed, it is said the locals in Loppington still persisted in bull baiting for another 18 months or so until the law clamped down on them.

Here, some local boys have been persuaded by photographer Bob Craig to go with the "challenge to a fight" angle. Leslie Williams, aged 10, is turning over the ring, challenging his school pals who are William Williams, 11, John Shakespeare, eight, and John Jenkins, also eight. Loppington is a very pleasant village three and a half miles west of Wem in north Shropshire. Bull baiting was apparent practised until around 1835. Bears were also baited here, it pains this author to report. And the last bear-baiting was the highlight of revelries that followed the marriage of the vicar's daughter in 1825.

The Royal Oak at Cardington, one of England's oldest pubs, is seen here in July 1959. According to some the man pictured is Hector Roberts, of Gretton, who was one of the drivers of Boulton Coaches, based in the village. He is probably on his way home from the garage for lunch. But another name suggested is that of Mr Eric Hall. The Royal Oak had an unexpected royal visitor on a snowswept January day in 1986 when Prince Edward used the pub as "base camp" for six hours of filming in the hills nearby. He returned afterwards to the pub, where the landlord only had 15 minutes' notice of his arrival. He warmed up in front of the fire and chose a speciality from the menu – Shropshire Fidget Pie, which is best gammon cooked with apples and onion in a bit of cider and some Worcester sauce. Afterwards the pub had phone calls and letters from people all over the country asking for the recipe. To commemorate the visit, there is a picture of the prince sitting in front of the fireplace in the pub.

Shawbury old parish hall on February 26, 1968. As ever, there is a campaign under way to raise money for a "new community centre". You can see that the thermometer on the wall is near the top. A new parish hall was indeed built, almost entirely of wood. Any time now it is expected to be demolished and replaced with an entirely new parish hall for the 21st century.

"Mid-Shropshire magistrates courts have now ceased to be held at Pontesbury police station, where they have functioned since about 1893. All the Mid-Salop sittings will now be held at the Shirehall, Shrewsbury," said the original caption to this photo, which dates from December 1963. The building is these days virtually unchanged, the home of Clifford Challinor (Assurance) Ltd. The cells downstairs are still there, complete with the cell doors with the old slats which were pulled down to put the food trays through. The company uses the cells for storing files.

This photograph of the Diddlebury Dip in July 1960 turns out to have captured two generations of a south Shropshire farming family. Brian Corfield is on the tractor and his father Sydney is walking on the bridge, with their dog Trudi trotting ahead. Brian was most probably going thistle cutting. The family came to Church Farm, the white house near the church, in 1937, moving from Hill End, at the end of the Long Mynd. The van may have been owned by Price the butcher. Diddlebury church in the distance is one of the oldest in England, and some of the distinctive Saxon craftmanship survives.

Pupils of Chirbury Church of England Primary School at play outside the School House which was built in 1675 on part of the old churchyard. Because of parishioners' rights, a settlement was made that the headteacher paid one shilling per year and was obliged to provide four Sunday services a year. This photograph is from 1972.

Only the fashions and cars are clues to the age of this picture. It's Cressage and we would have to say late sixties, early seventies.

A Working County

EVERYONE takes photographs these days. Virtually every home has a camera. And certainly ever since, say, the 1950s, people have taken – if not pictures of everyday occurrences – then at least holiday snaps at Blackpool or Bournemouth or Barmouth.

So if you wanted to compile a book now about seaside breaks over the past half century, you would have a wealth of material from which to choose.

You'd be spoilt for choice!

But – and here's a question – just how many of us take photographs of people at work?

For such images we rely almost exclusively upon newspapers or else official pictures taken by companies and organisations.

So this section then features some truly unusual shots that somehow manage to make the ordinary extraordinary.

There's a road repair crew in Woore in the early part of the 20th century, threshing at a farm near All Stretton in 1953, and an impressive line-up of lorries outside the premises of South Shropshire Farmers in the sixties.

And there are also hairdressers, potato pickers, cabinet makers, and many more besides.

So if you should be thinking about taking up photography as a hobby, don't neglect the wealth of subjects available out there in the workplace!

A road works gang in Woore. The picture is undated, but it must be from the early 20th century. The photograph was turned into a postcard and the message on the back of it read: "Dear Fred, Hoping to find you all well… We had these PC took the other day. A village in Shropshire. There is only two of us in this gang. Let me have a PC on return quick. 64 Shrewsbury Road, Market Drayton, Salop." *Picture: Ray Farlow.*

A wonderfully atmospheric shot. Threshing at Botvyle, All Stretton, in 1953. *Picture: S.R. Turner.*

Women workers leave a strike meeting for Clifford Williams employees held at the Park Road Club, Dawley, on November 10, 1972. Nearly 500 women workers at the Clifford Williams plants at Dawley and Madeley walked out on unofficial strike after the firm, which made clothing, employed a part-time woman worker at the Dawley factory. Later they voted to return to work. The Dawley factory had opened in 1955. It was originally known as Pyjamas Ltd, and some people locally continued to call it by this old name.

Our little joke. Those of you who bought our book *Shrewsbury: Pictures From The Past* will recognise this photograph as having appeared in that book's pages captioned as being the engine sheds at Coleham. Readers were not slow to point out that these were in fact the engine sheds at Oswestry. So here they are again! *Picture: Shropshire Records and Research Centre.*

Cliff Cotton, who took this photograph from a mound behind the Lilleshall Company's Snedshill Brickworks, did so because he was struck by the proliferation of chimneys, both in the foreground and in the distance. The date is uncertain, but may be around 1949. The brickworks are in the foreground, and upper left are Priorslee Furnaces. They were Shropshire's last remaining blast furnaces in operation, and were closed in 1959 after 107 years. The site has been completely cleared and modern offices stand there now. The closure of Snedshill Brickworks after 164 years was announced in 1966. Many of the buildings in the foreground remain today, but most of the chimney stacks have disappeared or been truncated and the derelict area in the distance is dominated by the Telford Plaza block and Telford town centre.

An impressive line-up of lorries at the South Shropshire Farmers base in June 1969.

The accounts department of the South Shropshire Farmers Ltd at the same time.

Brian Ball of Ketley at work at the Lilleshall Company steel rolling mill in February 1971, two days before his 17th birthday. The mill was in the Priorslee-Snedshill area. "The steel ingot in the picture was stainless steel and was to be rolled into billets for Wilkinson Sword of Sheffield. They would then make it into razor blades," says Brian, who is not identified by name on the original caption, but who recognised himself after seeing this photo. "The money as a young man was very good at £40 to £50 a week."

Mr Frank Ashley of Cordwell Park, Wem, tries out the new vacuum-operated street sweeper in the main street of Wem in June 1970.

A typical view of industry in the 1960s. This is Audco Ltd at Newport.

And here is the company again, as Serck Audco, in April 1969. The firm had twin factories at Audley Road and Audley Avenue, and the 900 workers produced 400,000 valves – and we're talking industrial valves for pipelines and so on – a year for the home and export market. The firm had started as a small cycle and farm machinery workshop and then in 1906 the Audley Engineering Company was formed. It became Audco – a contraction of the words Audley and Company – in 1961, and then in 1968 became Serck-Audco to reflect the links with the 12-firm combine of the Birmingham-based Serck Radiator Group. It was once Newport's biggest employer, but closed at the end of July 1999.

On January 2, 1961, Bishop's Castle's first ever factory opened. The Plaza cinema, which had closed a few months before, was bought by E.R. Hammersley and Co Ltd of Cradley Heath and, at the cost of £6,000, it was turned into a clothing factory. The local council had been working for several years to try to attract industry to the agricultural market town. This picture was taken a few days after the opening of the factory, which employed 37 women and girls at first, but had big expansion plans. For workers who lived outside Bishop's Castle, the company operated a special bus to bring them in.

Lorries and trailers loaded with sugar beet lining up outside the sugar factory at Allscott on January 31, 1979. There was a crisis in the sugar beet industry at the time and these lorries were part of a queue of up to 30 waiting to get inside, causing severe traffic problems on the roads. A high proportion of the loads were being turned away because the crop was frost damaged. On one day, 216 loads were accepted but another 168 were rejected, and Shropshire farmers were losing hundreds of pounds. The sugar beet plant at Allscott is one of Shropshire's oldest agricultural businesses. Production started there in 1927.

Tern Hill Garage, probably around 1930. It stood on the A41 and was demolished in the mid-1930s. The entrance to RAF Tern Hill – now the Army's Clive Barracks – is at or near the spot now. On the motorcycle is Frank Chatham, who started working at the garage as a mechanic in about 1928. Behind him is Arthur Hankey, who was also a mechanic. The cars are, from left, a Graham Paige, a Rover, and a Bull Nose Morris. *Picture: Frank Chatham.*

A line of machinists working on the garment section at the Laura Ashley factory on the Maesbury Road industrial estate at Oswestry on November 15, 1979. The plant there had been opened in March 1977 with about 20 machinists. At the time of this picture it employed 165 people, and more jobs were on the way when the firm took over a second factory to house the expanding soft furnishings section. The company was celebrating its 25th year and was described as "one of the biggest success stories of the British fashion industry". Of late, Laura Ashley has been having a more torrid time. It pulled out of Oswestry around Christmas 1998.

The powerhouse of industry. A view across the fields to Ironbridge Power Station from Coalbrookdale in 1962 or 1963. This is the original Ironbridge "A" Power Station, which was opened in 1932 by Mr P.J. Pybus, the Minister of Transport. Built initially with three chimneys, with its gleaming brasswork and reliability it was nicknamed the Queen Mary by workers. Later a further three chimneys were added. When the new "B" power station was built in the 1960s, the "A" station continued in operation, and was able to have a laugh at the teething troubles of the brash newcomer. It was finally demolished in the early 1980s.

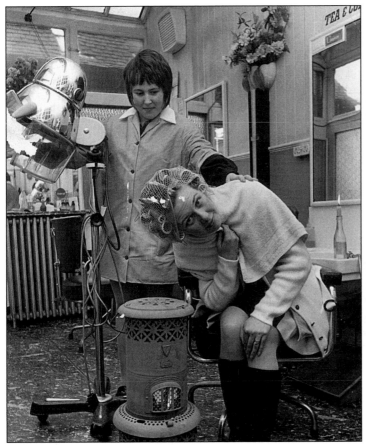

Although this particular picture was unidentified when trawled from the *Shropshire Star* vaults, we have reason to believe it is Mr M.S. Walker's Norton Farm at Upton Magna in the mid-1960s as potato picking gets under way.

Permanent waves were nothing new at ladies hairdressing salons, even back in February 1972, but how about this paraffin perm at an Oswestry salon? A power cut caused Mrs Irene Brayne of Kinnerley, near Oswestry, to go over this paraffin stove instead of under the electric hair drier. But fortunately the power supply was soon restored.

Aerial spraying at Mr Lea's Steppes Farm at Childs Ercall in September 1967. Flying at 40ft to 50ft, the plane is spraying ICI chalk fertiliser on a field of rape. The watching throng appears to be standing on part of the old Childs Ercall airfield.

Girls at work in Clifford Williams' Dawley factory in November 1970.

Women at work in the Hadley premises rented by Link 51 Ltd, assembling industrial lockers. The scene is from April 1970.

The general machine shop at Davies & Metcalfe, Oswestry, on August 29, 1969. The engineering firm was based at the old Cambrian Works, the former Oswestry headquarters of the Cambrian Railways. It was a specialist in making air brakes for wagons and locomotives. And it was one of the first to make the insides for automatic doors. In the late 60s and early 70s it had a thriving football team. Sadly the firm closed in the mid 1970s.

The Oakengates Urban District Council Sewage Disposal Works at Trench in 1969.

Midland Poultry Holdings Ltd, at Craven Arms, in July 1969.

IT MADE THE NEWS

A QUIET backwater? Maybe that's how the London-based journalists view Shropshire. We are, of course, quite a long way beyond that Watford horizon.

But we know differently, don't we?

Contrary to what you may have read in the national papers, who can't believe anything of significance happens away from the capital, the longest peacetime siege in recent British history happened near Wem in 1968. They prefer to think that it was the one on their doorstep, at Hackney, in January 2003.

There have been high-profile crimes. The Hilda Murrell mystery comes to mind. In the 1980s, COD Donnington was hit by two fires, in 1983 and 1988, which must have been among the most expensive in British peacetime history. The total cost was well over £300 million. As they were blamed on arsonists, it follows they were probably the most expensive arsons in history.

And so on. But news isn't just tragedy and disaster. It's the little things too, those little events which form the tapestry of everyday life.

As most of the pictures in this book are newspaper pictures, they arguably all fall into the category of "news". Here is a selection. Take a peek at the proof that Shropshire isn't as quiet as some think. It all happens here!

It was in the evening of May 9, 1967, that a runaway lorry carrying a load of rock ploughed into a row of cottages in Shineton Street, Much Wenlock, the driver leaping from his cab in the nick of time. Inside, Mr Edward Merrick, 64, and his wife Louisa were in the kitchen when the vehicle burst through the wall and into their front room. But happily they, together with 35-year-old lorry driver George Smith, of Church Road, Trench, escaped unhurt. In those days traffic approached down a hill directly towards the cottages. It was an accident waiting to happen – the road layout was changed afterwards. The lorry was carrying its load four miles from the Ridge Lime quarry to a dam being built at Devils Dingle. Mr Smith, a father of three, said "As I approached the corner I changed into low fourth gear. But when I touched the brakes nothing happened. I slammed the lorry into third, and then second gear and tried to swing it into a wall beside the cottage." About four yards from impact he jumped, and then ran into the premises to see if anyone was hurt. As an aside, Shineton Street is one of those addresses with an uncertain spelling. It says Shineton Street on the sign at one end, and Sheinton Street – which is more logical, because Sheinton is the name of a nearby village – at the other.

Hollywood actress Jennifer Jones during the filming of the Mary Webb book *Gone To Earth* in Much Wenlock in 1949. The picture looks like it was taken in front of The Guildhall, which was used in the location shooting. The person on the left is unidentified. Over 300 Shropshire people were recruited locally as extras, including members of Wenlock Players. The production team set up base at the Long Mynd Hotel in Church Stretton and The Regal cinema in Church Stretton was used to view the newly filmed sequences. Locations used included Much Wenlock, Longnor Hall, Lord's Hill chapel, Snailbeach, the Stiperstones, Eyton-on-Severn, Pontesford Hill, and Ludlow. A hangar at Sleap airfield was turned into a film studio. Sadly, some sequences shot in Shropshire were either cut from the final film or reshot in London. The provincial premiere was in Shrewsbury's Granada Cinema in October 1950.

There was talk two or three years ago of a remake starring Daniel Day-Lewis, but it has remained just talk to date. Nevertheless, the original film is now available on DVD. The critics were not kind. "A disaster, except for Jennifer Jones' performance," and "unintentionally funny," were just some of the comments.

This is a picture which went around the world – taken a split second before the gunman opened fire at the *Shropshire Star* photographer. Johnnie Johnson was training his long lens on a house in the wilds of north Shropshire where a gunman was holed up. "I was looking at the windows to see if I could see him and when I got to this centre window it was open, he appeared at the window, pointed his gun and fired at myself and a detective. I couldn't believe it. I just managed to get one frame and I was off down the lane faster than the bullet came out of that gun," said Johnnie. Although a more recent 15-day Hackney siege was billed by the London papers as Britain's longest, the Shropshire standoff at Weston-under-Redcastle in 1968 was longer, with gunman John James holding police and the Army at bay for 17 days. James later claimed that he had fired because he thought Johnnie was a policeman with a gun – a plausible mistake, as Johnnie had a 200mm long lens with a pistol grip. The Army advanced on the house, but quickly retreated when James shot the aerial off their armoured car. The siege ended when a hostage grabbed the gun. This scoop snap went into the Commonwealth Picture Competition. It came second.

Death of a royal. Prince William of Gloucester died shortly after takeoff from Halfpenny Green airfield on August 28, 1972. He was taking part in an air race. His aircraft was in a steep left hand turn but never pulled out, and came down in Six Ashes Lane, almost exactly on the Shropshire-Staffordshire border, not far from the Royal Oak pub, Bobbington. His co-pilot was also killed. This picture by Ray Bradbury of the *Express & Star*, the *Shropshire Star's* sister paper, won the Midland News Picture of the Year award.

"Neilson Wins" declare the posters on the front of "Neilson's Committee Room" in Hinstock, with a glimpse of Hinstock School in the background on the left. On the side of the building is a poster saying "Vote for Stanier". The date of this photograph is not known for certain but appears to be around 1910, give or take a couple of years. The car is a French one – a de Dion Bouton. Perhaps the gentleman standing by the car is Francis Neilson himself, a Liberal candidate who did electoral battle with Beville Stanier. But the "Neilson Wins" posters are very puzzling. In the

Newport Division election of May 1908 he was beaten by Stanier, the Unionist candidate, by 951 votes. In the previous general election of January 1906, Neilson had also lost, this time by 176 votes against Colonel Kenyon-Slaney, the Conservative candidate. And in the two 1910 general elections, Beville Stanier won one against a different opponent, and was returned unopposed in the other. Perhaps the answer is that the posters were a bit of Edwardian hype, associating Neilson with success which he did not in the event achieve. *Picture: Alf Evans.*

Goodbye to Tong Castle on July 18, 1954. The demolition of the 18th-century building was done with a certain amount of ceremony before a crowd of hundreds of people. Lord Newport, on whose estate the ruins stood, pressed the button which fired the charges placed around the base of the building by sappers of the 125 Company, Royal Engineers, T.A., from Cannock, commanded by Lt Col A.P. Daniell. They thought it would be a useful exercise to benefit their training. An observer wrote: "In a split second the sandstone façade had disappeared in a great cloud of reddish smoke and dust to leave a heap of rubble which Lord Newport said would be put to many uses on the estate. Officers of the unit thought the 'big bang' could not have gone more smoothly." The building was demolished because Lord Newport and Shifnal Rural Council agreed that it was unsafe. Some years previously a youth had slipped when climbing over this once popular rendezvous for sightseers from all over the country and he was killed. What remained after the demolition was destroyed by the building of the M54 motorway. For Shropshire people, the last chance most had of seeing what was left was in 1981, when archaeologists opened up the site to hundreds of visitors. Then the diggers moved in.

It looks like the Blitz, but it was in fact the aftermath of a gas explosion at Temeside, Ludlow, on April 19, 1973. The blast ripped through a row of houses. Apart from the two homes which were demolished, two others and an office block were damaged. Two people were seriously hurt and others had amazing escapes. A family of seven escaped unhurt after dashing down a blazing staircase. In the aftermath there was a big row, with residents claiming they had been reporting the smell of gas for months previously, but the gas board was adamant that the only alert they had had came 20 minutes before the explosion, and they had been on their way when the blast happened. Amid the anger there was also compassion. Local people and firms rallied round to help those who had lost everything. The demolished properties were not rebuilt. It was not Ludlow's last explosion. Eighteen months later Temeside was rocked by another gas blast which demolished a bungalow.

Farmworker Ray Williams only just failed to beat the world cheese-eating record at his local pub in Ruyton-XI-Towns in November 1971. Ray, of Birch Grove, Ruyton-XI-Towns, is seen attempting to eat a pound of cheddar cheese in 11 minutes 22 seconds, but when the time was up he had managed to get through only 14 ounces. Nevertheless, he still managed to raise £15 for charity. Later exploits by Ray "Willpower" Williams included pulling a bus with his teeth.

Over 200 children at the Grove Comprehensive School at Market Drayton ran out of school on December 17, 1970, to demonstrate through the town in support of their drama master, Mr R.G. "Greg" Gregory. The master had been sacked by Salop education committee for failing to comply with the school's articles of government. Chanting slogans of "We Want Greg", and waving banners and posters, the pupils formed up in the school playground and then rushed up Stafford Street into Shropshire Street. Traffic came to a standstill and shoppers stood and stared. Masters hurriedly dispatched from the school turned the children back. When the main body returned to the school they stood and shouted their slogans and catcalls round the office of the headmaster, Mr H.A. Behenna, who came out to talk to them.

The Weston Lullingfields School closure protesters are pictured arriving at the Shirehall, Shrewsbury, in May 1976.

Shropshire summer school for secondary modern teachers, being held in Shrewsbury, visited the Roman villa at Yarchester, near Much Wenlock, in July 1958. A mosaic floor had been uncovered at the site in the shadow of the Wenlock Edge. The excavation had been done by staff and pupils at Much Wenlock Secondary Modern School, led by renowned local archaeologist Mr W.A. Silvester, who had apparently pinpointed the site by investigating the habits of the moles in the field, which surfaced in lines indicating the outline of the Roman villa. Eventually the excavated site was covered over again to preserve the relics.

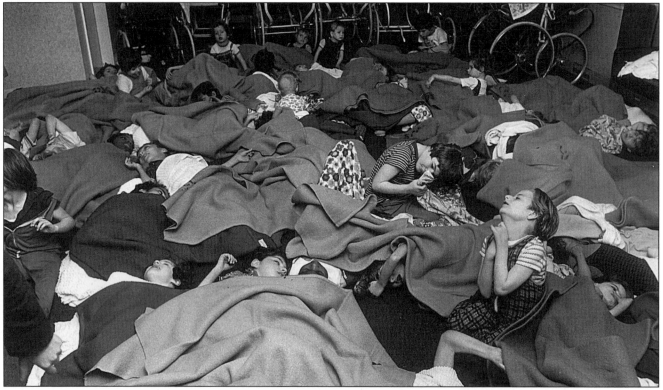

Safe and sound… Eighty-one severely physically and mentally handicapped children rest in the day room of Loppington House, near Wem, after a fire raged through the building, a privately run nursing home, before dawn on July 14, 1976. The children were snatched to safety by a human chain of staff – still in their nightclothes – firefighters, and ambulance personnel. Some of the children were at first feared trapped, but within minutes all were accounted for. They ranged from a few months old to 12 years old. The only casualty was an auxiliary nurse who suffered from the effects of smoke and shock.

Firefighters battle to save top canoeist Brian Springthorpe, who was trapped in his kayak when it smashed into a fallen tree on the River Severn at Ironbridge, not far from the Bedlam Furnaces, on February 9, 1977. He and his canoeing companion Kenneth Morris were in training for an international race being held at Llangollen when they came to grief in the icy, fast-flowing waters of the Severn. Morris was thrown clear and swam to safety, but 20-year-old Brian was pinned. It took a six-hour rescue operation involving over a dozen firefighters and a mobile crane with a 92ft jib to free him. Firefighters got him to sing dirty songs and slapped his face to keep him conscious during the operation. Brian, from Wednesfield, was treated at the Royal Salop Infirmary for exposure and leg injuries.

Repairs being carried out at the banks of the River Severn at Atcham in the aftermath of flood damage. The year is 1947.

It's March 1965 and here is Mrs Locke at Morville with three of her eight children. The accompanying story reads: "While gipsy families like this go on living in their caravans and tents, it was revealed today that Shropshire is to take part in a nationwide probe into problems created by these nomadic people."

A student protest march sets up camp at Lord Hill's Column near the Shirehall, Shrewsbury, in November 1976. Organisers explained that the protest was peaceful and not disruptive. More than one hundred protesters from Shrewsbury Technical College (Tech), later renamed Shrewsbury College of Arts and Technology (SCAT) on London Road, took part in a national day of action over education cuts. After handing in a petition to assistant education officer John Till, they set out to carry on their demonstration. Trouble nearly began when they were told by security officials and the police to stop climbing over the stone lions at the foot of the column. The students had earlier made a half-hearted attempt to stop traffic in Abbey Foregate by a sitdown protest.

A dole queue in Oswestry in May 1970. A sensitive time – the general election was looming.

Lady Diana Spencer has a day out at Ludlow races on October 24, 1980. This "elegant blonde" was said to be "the latest in a long line of royal girlfriends". She was at the races to watch Prince Charles romp home second on his horse Allibar in the Clun Amateur Riders Handicap Chase. The 19-year-old future Princess of Wales pictured by a *Shropshire Star* photographer on that day was the centre of attention, but her friend and companion on the right did not attract much interest. She was, in fact, Camilla Parker-Bowles, and this is a rare photograph of the pair together. The gentleman is unidentified but may be trainer Nick Gaselee.

School staff carry baskets of linen from the blazing Ellesmere College on June 23, 1966. Fire ripped through the college during the evening. Smoke was seen seeping from the gabled day room in the centre of the north wing at about 7pm and within minutes the fire had spread, sending up a plume of smoke visible six miles away. The flames gripped the wing containing the dining room and chapel. Over 50 firefighters fought for hours to stop the fire spreading, relaying water from the pond in the school grounds and the boys' swimming pool. Hundreds of people watched the drama.

And this was the aftermath of the Ellesmere College fire. Only the walls of the wing were left standing. Happily nobody was hurt. Little was saved, apart from some altar silver and choristers' robes. Royal Artillery soldiers from Park Hall Camp, Oswestry, provided blankets and served breakfast for the boys as they sat on the golf course. And despite the disaster, which was blamed on an electrical fault, the wing was to rise phoenix-like from the ashes. Less than three years later, on May 17, 1969, the rebuilt wing was opened by former Minister of Education Sir Edward Boyle and the Bishop of Stepney, the Rt Rev Trevor Huddleston. The cost of the rebuilding was about £250,000.

Residents of the village of Alberbury wait to sign the petition protesting at Salop County Council's proposal to close the village's 100-year-old primary school and instead send the children to Ford School some miles away. Putting his name to the petition here is Mr J.M. Llewellyn, of Upper Houses, Alberbury. It is August 1964.

Deputy Mayor of Bishop's Castle, Councillor W.H. Jarvis, and his 16-year-old daughter Gwyneth, led a contingent from the town to the opening of a boundary review inquiry at the Shirehall in Shrewsbury in June 1964. The inquiry threatened to see the end of England's smallest borough. The battle to save the independence of Bishop's Castle failed. The last civic parade of Bishop's Castle Borough Council was held in 1966 and on April 1, 1967, a major council shake-up saw the end of borough councils at Ludlow, Oswestry and Bishop's Castle.

The scene at Church Street, Broseley, on January 23, 1975, where partly demolished buildings had brought complaints from residents that the ruins were dangerous because children had been using the site as a playground and were throwing bricks and rubble about. The partly demolished buildings were numbers 15, 15a, and 16 Church Street, once a shop and cottages. Contractors had moved in the previous autumn, but apparently left the site in this state after five weeks. Bridgnorth District Council had finally stepped in to give them 28 days to clear the site.

Midland Red bus driver John Pryce stamped on his brakes and his bus slithered to a halt at the edge of a collapsed bridge just outside the village of Withington, near Shrewsbury, on February 25, 1969. Only minutes earlier he had crossed the same canal bridge. But on the way back, it simply wasn't there. This picture taken at the scene on the day of the incident shows him puzzling over his lucky escape. The bus, which had by that time been reversed up the road, is in the background. The road was temporarily closed, and the gap was filled in with rubble.

Severe flooding grips Bridgnorth on January 16, 1968. There was a belief that new reservoirs built in Mid Wales would prevent flooding of the River Severn. Events have proven it to be a misconception.

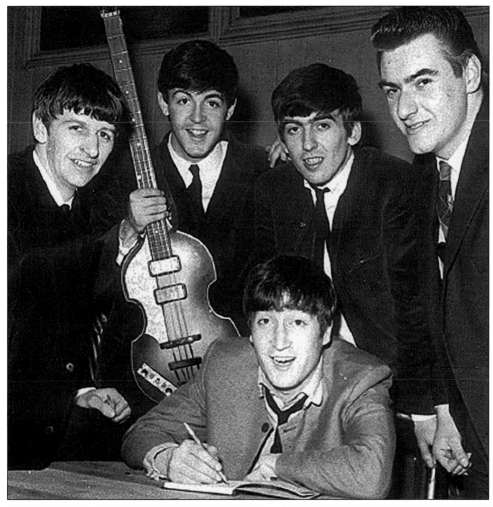

In 1965 they were at Buckingham Palace to receive their MBEs. In 1966, with their popularity reaching unprecedented levels, John Lennon was forced to conclude controversially: "The Beatles are bigger than Jesus Christ." In 1967, The Sunday Times called them "the greatest composers since Beethoven." They still hold the record for the most number one hits while their much-loved, much-respected and groundbreaking LPs continue to feature among the very highest positions in polls for the greatest ever albums. But before any of this, The Beatles played at the Music Hall, Shrewsbury. This was on December 14, 1962. Local fan Chris Wallace knew the bouncer and got him and his brother David Wallace upstairs to the changing rooms to get their autographs. Dave got the lads to sign the back of his students' union card and autograph book. The man on the right – not one of the Wallaces – is thought to be the Music Hall manager. The Beatles were back in Shrewsbury the following year. They played at the Granada on February 28, and at the Music Hall, for the second time, on April 26. *Picture: David Wallace.*

The Hotel, on the corner of Sandford Avenue in the centre of Church Stretton, was the scene of one of Shropshire's saddest fire tragedies. In the late evening of April 2, 1968, five people died, including three children. It happened within weeks of another disastrous fire, at Shelton Hospital, in which 24 patients died. The children were brothers – twins aged seven, and a nine-year-old – who had been staying at the 40-bedroomed three-star hotel with their parents for one night as they prepared to move in to their new home in Shrewsbury Road, Church Stretton, the following day. Their parents were rescued by firefighters. The others who died were an 18-year-old waitress at the hotel, and a maid.

Firefighters in the charred main lobby of The Hotel, where the fire was thought to have started. In more recent times, the building has housed a variety of uses, including a travel agency.

A Wolverhampton Corporation double-decker bus, No. 17, travelling into Bridgnorth, has got stuck beneath the ancient town hall in High Street. The bus had set down its passengers in West Castle Street. Normally, it should have turned round for its return to Wolverhampton at Postern Gate instead of travelling up High Street. It was eventually released after the tyres had been deflated. There was little damage. The date? May 30, 1967.

The old Butter Cross at Claverley was undergoing renovation by a Bridgnorth firm of stonemasons in February 1965. Only one new piece of stone was being used, the rest being reclaimed from the surrounds. This type of stone, originally quarried at Alveley, was no longer available. Here an agricultural conveyor is being used to take the pieces of masonry to the top.

The "new" three-forked pole of Clee Hill was erected in July 1972 and despite pouring rain and thick mist, more than 100 people turned up to witness the event. The pole that this one replaced was said to be more than 300 years old and marked the point where three parishes met – Corley, Bitterley, and Hopton Wafers. In the picture, Mr Priest, a parish councillor of Corley, takes away the chains to allow the new pole to stand on its own. *Picture: G.H. Davies.*

A young pupil at the Condover Hall School for the Blind gets the feel of the splendour of a royal Rolls-Royce as the car stood waiting in the courtyard of the school during a royal visit on October 13, 1970. Princess Margaret went to the school to open a new £230,000 block of flats constructed to enable the staff and children to take part in a "family life" system which had been introduced in the school. The princess caused a mild sensation with her "with-it" outfit that day, which was said to have attracted gasps of admiration from parents and staff. It was described as a "mid-grey two-piece midi suit, wide-brimmed hat and the latest wet-look knee-length boots with chromium-plated heels."

On April 22, 1970, two Sioux helicopters on a training flight from RAF Tern Hill collided while they were flying in formation near Hinstock. Both crashed, coming down about 200 yards apart in fields at Lockley Wood. The pilots were flown to hospital. Second from the right is Group Captain James Corbishley, commanding officer of RAF Tern Hill, who flew to the scene.

Back in February 1975 residents of Weir Cottages, Hanwood, handed Shrewsbury's mayor Councillor Tom Ryder a petition in a bid to stop numbers 6 to 24 being knocked down. The council had decided the cottages should not be re-let as they became vacant and that they should eventually be demolished. The petition asking the council to reconsider was signed by several hundred people. From left: Miss Beatrice Redge, Mr John Redge, Mr Harry Bowers, Mr Maurice Jones, and Mr Vincent Spragg.

Gobowen villagers were just about getting over their Christmas festivities when a fire began in the afternoon of December 27, 1979, at All Saints Church. Five hours later, when firefighters from all over Shropshire had brought it under control, the 50-year-old church was a ruined, roofless shell. Here Mr Albert Pearse and the vicar, the Rev John Allen, get about the business of clearing up the site on March 16, 1980. An appeal was already under way to restore the church, and by this date had raised more than £15,000. The appeal succeeded and the restored church was rededicated on October 3, 1981.

Some of the bidders at an auction of the remaining part of the former Royal Naval storage depot at Ditton Priors. They were at Ditton Priors Village Hall on November 17, 1971, where a final 10 lots came under the hammer, including the storage and administrative site, the station yard, and land which could be redeveloped. The sale was conducted by Ludlow auctioneers McCartney, Morris and Barker on behalf of the Secretary of State for Defence and the lots went for a total of £47,950.

August 1965 – "Warning notices were put up this morning at Ellesmere Mere, one of Shropshire's beauty spots, after a freak landslide last night in which a bulldozer driver escaped death by inches. Jim Edwards, 27, of Tetchill, married with two children, was using his five-ton bulldozer to level soil at the side of the lake when he noticed cracks appearing in the ground. He got clear and seconds later, thousands of tons of soil crumbled away from the mereside into the water. Water rushed in to fill the gap and an island of mud appeared. A car park and picnicking spot have completely disappeared into the lake. So have three large trees. Engineers who visited the scene fear that further subsidence could threaten the main Ellesmere-Whitchurch road which is less than 20 yards from the lake."

More than 300 residents of Craven Arms drowned out a priest speaking on behalf of gipsies at this public meeting in October 1974. Salop County Council had plans for a 12-caravan site in the town. Father Maxwell from Liverpool was explaining how similar problems of gipsy sites were overcome in his area. But he was not allowed to finish. The county's scheme had sparked off a major protest from locals. All five parish councils in the area combined to oppose the plan.

Hole lot of trouble. In August 1973 council officials and a building firm were trying to solve the mystery of a hole in the ground which had opened up on a Shrewsbury building site, bringing work to a halt. The hole was 6ft wide at the mouth, broadening in a bottleneck shape to 20ft wide, and was known to be at least 18ft deep. It stopped work on a small number of houses on the Castlefields site of Watkin, Starbuck and Jones while an investigation got under way to try to find out what it was.

The aftermath of a devastating fire which hit the Robert Jones and Agnes Hunt Orthopaedic Hospital at Gobowen on January 27, 1948. Despite the rapidity of the blaze, nurses and helpers saved all of the 500 to 600 patients before the fire reached their wards. The hospital had been set up at the former Park Hall military hospital in 1921. It was rebuilt after the fire. It was not a good year for the hospital – which is also often called Shropshire Orthopaedic Hospital. In the autumn, there was a typhoid epidemic there. Seven died and over 100 were infected in the outbreak, which began in September 1948 and ended on October 23. The cause was not discovered for certain, but contaminated milk was suspected.

The Bird 'n' B's pop group from Shropshire were on the brink of fame in the 1960s. This publicity picture was taken at a playground somewhere in Trench. The members were, from left: Mick Skinner, of Trench, guitar; Chris Wallace, of Donnington, singer; Dawn Cullis, from Dawley (now Dawn Rice of Shifnal), drummer; Jim Wilkie, of Donnington, bass; and Gerry Ward of Wellington, guitar. Dawn recalls that Ludlow Town Hall was the venue for a Beat Groups competition. "We won our heat and went on to win the final. We had many supporters – a fan club in Shropshire, and also in Staffordshire, both of whom would bring coachloads of fans to see us. I'm sure there are lots of Shropshire people who will remember this event as fondly as I do. The Bird 'n' B's turned professional as a result of winning this competition." The group was renamed Fluff in November 1968 and Dawn left soon after. The Shropshire popstars hovered on the brink of stardom, but never quite made it. *Picture: Dawn Rice.*

Mr Frank Davies, chairman of the managers of Lyneal School, hands over a petition to Oswestry MP John Biffen calling for the school to be spared from closure, as placard-carrying youngsters look on. Most residents of Lyneal had signed the petition objecting against the closure plans, and Mr Biffen was taking up the case on their behalf. Lyneal School was one of a number of primary schools in Shropshire lined up for the axe by the county council, in a move aimed at saving £5,000 a year.

Shortly before pub closing time on November 15, 1972, a lorry ploughed into the crowded Greyhound Inn alongside the A5 in Ketley Bank. Lorry driver David Lewis, 24, of Knighton, was hauled from his crushed cab seconds before the bar roof caved in. Five people were hurt. The pub was so badly damaged it had to be virtually rebuilt.

In the immediate post-war period RAF Shawbury was the centre of a number of record-breaking long distance flights, called the "Aries" flights, after the name of the Lancaster aircraft involved. Here the crew of Aries line up in front of the plane on January 15, 1946, before flying to South Africa. Aries took off from Shawbury at 2.35 pm on this day for Thorney Island, en route to South Africa. Air Commodore N.H. D'Aeth CBE commandant of the Empire Air Navigation School at Shawbury, flew as officer in charge of the mission. The captain of the Aries was Wing Commander C. Dunnicliffe, DSO, DFC, from Paisley, Scotland, and whose home was at Fritwell, Bicester.

Other members of the crew were Flight Lieutenant G.G. Taylor, DFC, second pilot of St Stephens, St Austell; Captain M.H. Short, South African Air Force, first navigator, of Johannesburg; Flt Lt J.H. Frewemn (*sic*), second navigator of Rhodesia; Flt Lt H.S. Heitz, first wireless operator of 69 Oakfield Road, Copthorne, Shrewsbury; Sergeant C. Horrocks, second wireless operator of Bolton; Flying Officer H.B.F. Biddle, engineering officer of 23 Chapel Lane, Codsall, Wolverhampton; Sergeant R. Schofield, Flight Engineer of Rochdale; youngest member of the crew was 22-year-old Sergeant L. Swinden, electrician, who came from Wakefield and whose home was in Shrewsbury; and Sergeant A.E. Creasey, radar mechanic of Leicester.

The sign indicates the position of the police office in Shifnal. On the other side of the road is the shop, Young and Upton Ltd., from which about £120 worth of stock was taken in a smash and grab raid early in the morning of August 5, 1964.

Oswestry cattle market was at the epicentre of the devastating epidemic of foot and mouth disease which broke out in October 1967. The photograph probably dates from October 26, the very start of the outbreak. The previous day a farmer at nearby Nantmawr had called in a vet to examine a sow and piglets. The vet suspected foot and mouth disease and an immediate standstill order was imposed over a five-mile radius, including the Oswestry smithfield, where earlier in the day the farmer had sent cattle to be sold. An immediate hunt began to trace the animals which had been sold at the market. Unfortunately it was too late to stop the spread of the disease. It was not until well into 1968 that the disease was conquered, at a cost of over £100 million and more than 421,000 animals slaughtered.

PLAYTIME

WHAT does a pillow fight at Hinstock in 1907 have in common with ladies playing bridge at Attingham Hall in 1965?

Playtime, of course!

We have no idea what percentage of all human endeavour is given over to simply having fun, but, you know what they say – All work and no play makes Jack a dull boy.

We have to let off steam or maybe just crash out from time to time. We have to find some time in our busy lives to just enjoy ourselves

And so it is that people down through the generations have played football, held swimming galas, fetes, carnivals and fairs, or else have formed amateur dramatics societies, bridge clubs, challenged one another to a game of tennis or golf or snooker. As they say – whatever turns you on.

In this section you'll see perfectly sane, grown-up people dressed in the style of the Elizabethans and standing on the backs of floats for no other reason than to put smiles on the faces of the crowds gathered at the roadside.

You'll see ladies at Hawkstone Park swimming pool in 1968 wearing frankly rather bizarre headgear. And then there are those rather earnest-looking gentlemen walking through the snow-covered grounds of Lilleshall Hall to play tennis back in the January of 1959.

While you're browsing (and perhaps at the same time) recalling your own misspent youth, don't miss the Bridgnorth youngsters enjoying a toboggan run in 1961 or the families enjoying the sunshine on the River Severn in the fifties.

Shrewsbury Flower Show – date unknown, but probably late 1940s or early 1950s. Stan Turner who took the picture says: "This aerial act had been introduced as a substitute for the high wire act which had been discontinued in the post-war years, but I omitted to date my negative."

Arthur Rowley creates an all-time British league scoring record with the 411th league goal of his career, with this shot at the Gay Meadow for Shrewsbury Town against Millwall on September 26, 1962. He broke the record set by Jimmy McGrory of Celtic. Rowley is in the dark shirt, just left of centre. It was not, of course, the last goal by the legendary Shrewsbury Town player. During a 19-year playing career, he hit the net 434 times in 619 league games. He finally hung up his boots in 1965 but stayed on at the Gay Meadow for three years as manager. Rowley died in December 2002.

Cyclists on a club run on March 18, 1951, at the top of Harley Bank, near Much Wenlock. *Picture: Bert Catchpole.*

This trio were among the many players taking part in a bridge party at Attingham Hall in aid of the NSPCC in February 1965.

Now, here's a real gem. It's the pillow fight at the flower show and sports event at Hinstock in 1907. The picture was loaned to us by Mr Alf Evans of Shrewsbury who was born in 1914 and whose parents were on the domestic staff at Hinstock Hall.

Shrewsbury Carnival in 1952. Mr Stan Turner who took this photograph says: "A float representing the Elizabethans passes along Mardol Quay towards Smithfield Road. The telephone box is on the site of the Hill's Arms pub which had been demolished to make way for the widening of Smithfield Road."

Rosie Pidwell, Caroline Craig, Nicky Cluff, Denise Whitby, and Gillian Mastyn in the Hawkstone Park swimming pool in June 1968.

The mother of the Mother of Parliament? Children play in the shadow of the Parliament Barn or Great Barn at Acton Burnell in July 1959. The barn may be the site of the first ever meeting of the first full English Parliament. Only the gable ends now remain of the Great Barn, in college fields close to the ruined Acton Burnell castle. The historic first parliament was summoned in Acton Burnell by Edward I in 1283, passing the Statute of Acton Burnell, a rather dull piece of legislation to do with payment of debts. Many historians think the barn was the meeting place and that it was even the residential hall where Edward I stayed, perhaps being relegated to storage once the nearby castle was completed.

The beginning of the jet age is evident in this view of RAF Shawbury's Battle of Britain celebrations in September 1954. Nearest the camera is a Canberra light bomber, one of the first military jet bombers, while beyond it is an Avro Lincoln, a version of the famous Avro Lancaster.

Carding Mill Valley at Church Stretton has always been a magnet for tourists. And here, during the Whitsun holiday of 1961, thousands of people crammed into the valley for picnics and walking. It was estimated that about 5,000 people, mostly from the Black Country, enjoyed a day out at the Shropshire beauty spot.

Lawn tennis in the snow. Teachers from various prep schools and public schools in the country enjoyed a training course at the National Recreation Centre at Lilleshall Hall in January 1959. The tennis training, though, took place in the covered King George VI Hall which accommodated two full-size courts.

It's time for winter sports! And making the most of what little snow there was on this afternoon in 1964 are these enthusiastic Bridgnorth youngsters. The steep pavements on the Hookfield estate proved ideal for a toboggan run.

Men simply don't wear hats like that any more, do they? (See the fella in the centre of the picture.) But apart from this small period detail as a clue, it's pretty hard to date this one. Any guesses? Well, actually, we know for a fact that it's August 1953 and it's families having fun on the River Severn at Bridgnorth.

Youngsters enjoying Market Drayton's outdoor pool in 1972.

A display of abseiling and confidence training by C Troop of the 24 (Irish) Battery, with members of the regimental PT staff, thrilled the many visitors to the Park Hall open day in May 1966.

Chris Fleming crosses the line well clear of the rest of the runners in Wem's pancake race on February 7, 1967.

Members of the Vine Angling Club, West Bromwich, chose the double bridges at Atcham, near Shrewsbury, for a morning's sport in October 1946.

The crowds were out at Clun to follow the carnival procession in August 1965.

When this photograph of the Midland Gliding Club's Long Mynd headquarters was taken from the air in December 1955 gale force winds were still driving snow into deep drifts which kept eight men and two women marooned on the hilltop. Look closely and you can see a couple of them waving to the photographer. The gliding club was formed in 1934 and stands close to the edge of a long west-facing ridge on the Long Mynd – the lip of the ridge is just beyond the club, running across the middle of the picture. The reason for choosing the site was that when the prevailing westerly winds hit the ridge they are deflected upwards, and in the right conditions gliders can stay aloft in the rising air for hours.

P. Goodwin of Haslington in his Shrike-Villiers go-kart takes the chequered flag in one of the heats at a go-kart meeting at Condover on April 19, 1965.

It's May Day and these children from Trefonen Church of England School are maypole dancing in the school playground. The year? 1968.

The main cast in the Ludlow Festival production of Shakespeare's *A Winter's Tale* are framed in this window of Ludlow Castle in June 1973. They are – from left – John Bown, Michael Elphick and Sebastian Graham Jones. Below: Ann Morrish, Jenny Twigge and Janet Key.

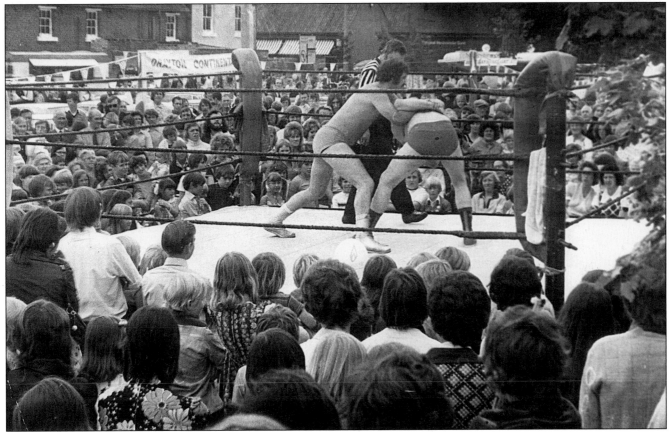

Crowds watch the wrestling bouts at Market Drayton Chamber of Trade's second Open Fair on the Queen Street car park, Market Drayton, in August 1974.

The inhabitants of the new old people's group dwellings at Broseley play cards at their party in February 1968. The warden, Mrs Nealley, said it was hoped to have a party on the first Thursday of every month.

Mr G.D. Stainsby, as Sir Despard Murgatroyd, during the dress rehearsal of Gilbert and Sullivan's *Ruddigore* by Oswestry Amateur Operatic Society at Oswestry Boys Modern School hall on January 2, 1967.

Driving tractors and smashing pianos were two of the attractions at Boningale Fair in June 1967. The fair was held on grounds opposite The Horns Inn. The highlight of the day was the tractor trials. The fair, held annually, is organised by the Horns of Boningale Club, to raise money for local charities.

Well, this recreational area looks like it needs a little attention, doesn't it? Bricks and rubble lying around while small children play? Wouldn't be allowed these days. It's 1968 and it's a playground at Wellington.

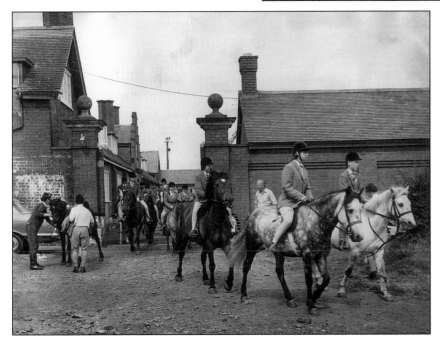

Members of the Ludlow Hunt branch of the National Pony Club at camp on Ludlow racecourse in August 1967.

SOMETHING LOST

IN our companion volumes to this book (*Shrewsbury: Pictures From The Past,* and *Telford: Pictures From The Past*), the many photographs of buildings that have since been bulldozed have been among the most poignant.

Perhaps it is part of the great unwritten mission of provincial newspapers to record these places before they vanish forever. Perhaps it is also part of the great unwritten mission of amateur photographers everywhere. For if these pictures are not taken then what is there left to speak for these places?

Not all historic structures are beautiful. Not all are grand or impressive.

Many are frankly bland and unremarkable. But nevertheless, all have their part to play and even the most mundane have usually worked themselves into the affections of the local population.

These days, if fine old buildings can be saved from demolition, they very often are. We are much more interested in and sympathetic to the concepts of preservation and conservation.

But sadly, in the 1960s and 1970s there was a trend for sweeping away the old in favour of the modern, even if the old was stylish and well-built while the modern was so often unimaginative and constructed of cheap materials.

In this section, let's pay our respects to Braggington Hall built in 1675, the Methodist Church at Broseley, Tern Hill railway station, and many others.

But the section is not only about buildings. It also looks at ways of life that have disappeared, retiring couples, aircraft on their last day in service, and even redundant water pumps!

Enjoy… and shed a tear.

Craven Arms Sunday School in 1932 or 1933 outside the old tin church in Corvedale Road, Craven Arms, which was taken down long ago. Mr Kenneth Plain is seventh from the left, front, and his lifelong friend Robert Corfield is eighth from left on the same row. *Picture: Kenneth Plain.*

Braggington Hall in Alberbury parish, photographed in 1962. Built in 1675, it was demolished shortly after this picture was taken. The site is now occupied by a modern bungalow! *Picture: S.R. Turner.*

The deserted control tower is a reminder of the best remembered years of Prees Heath, when it was host to a wartime bomber base. It and the hangars stand deserted and unwanted in this picture taken in May 1971. During the war the airfield was known initially as RAF Whitchurch Heath, and then, to avoid confusion with an airfield with a similar name, as RAF Tilstock. Today the busy A49 road carves through the middle of the site. Some of the hangars remain for storage, and the control tower also survives as a ruin.

NO LEFT TURN

NO ENTRY

NO RIGHT

NO ENTRY FOR SMITHFIELD TRAFFIC

THROUGH TRAFFIC TURN. LEFT

NO ENTRY

POLICE NO WAITING

Signs of the times at the Oswestry old police station – being used in 1969 as a rural borough council storeroom. The signs were no longer being used to direct traffic in Oswestry on Wednesdays (market day). Now that the new smithfield was open, the one-way traffic system had been discontinued. Stacking the signs is Mr John Marshall, an employee of the roads department.

Telephone "hello girls" from the Shrewsbury Telephone Exchange in 1953.

Pupils at Weston and Wixhill Church of England Primary School go to classes each day in a building certain to be steeped in architectural history, says the original 1972 caption to this picture. But – it goes on to say – "very little is known about its background, and the school governors and staff are trying to find out more… so far with little success. It appears to have been built more than 100 years ago by the land-owning family of Lord Hill."

The old Wem Corn and Seeds building with its "twin towers" was one of the distinctive landmarks of Wem. It all came to a fiery end late at night on Saturday, June 18, 1977, when flames gripped the premises, the former Maltings. Before long it was a raging inferno and the building in Station Road was completely destroyed. The blaze was said to have been the biggest in north Shropshire for years. Families were evacuated as 60 firemen tackled the flames which gutted the four-storey grain warehouse, destroying hundreds of tons of corn and seed. This photograph is undated, but doesn't look as if it can have been taken very long before the fire.

Not long now… These two cottages on Wem's High Street had survived the great 17th-century fire which caused so much damage to the town, but were in the sights of 20th-century councillors who wanted to get rid of them. They were considered an eyesore by members of North Shropshire Rural District Council back in 1968.

The Spreadeagles pub at Little Wenlock was about to close and disappear forever when this photograph was taken on or about December 30, 1958. The landlords were allowed to stay to pull one last pint, on December 31, 1958, before the pub was demolished virtually immediately to make way for the National Coal Board to mine the land beneath. The Spreadeagles was kept by a Mr and Mrs Phillip Wall. Mr Wall loved horse racing and trained racehorses. In his younger days he rode, and is said to have told how he had the distinction of winning a hurdle race, a chase, a flat race, and also at showjumping. Before the Walls the pub was kept by Bob Norgrove. In those days there were no pulls and they used to fetch the beer in jugs from down in the cellar.

The Wrekin beacon was the much-loved "friendly light" which flashed from the top of The Wrekin for generations. But it met its end in August 1970 when it was dismantled by nine airmen and three airwomen from RAF Shawbury. Ironically, they were doing it as their bit for European Conservation Year. The beacon was scrapped, according to contemporary reports, with proceeds going to the RAF Benevolent Fund. It had been installed in late 1942 or 1943 to stop aircraft crashing into The Wrekin, and was turned off in 1965, after which it fell derelict. Crowds gathered at the summit of The Wrekin on New Year's Eve, 1999, to watch as a new beacon was turned on to mark the new millennium. The new Wrekin beacon is actually two lights attached to the Wrekin telecommunications mast and has come in for some criticisms for unreliability and because older folk claim it is not as bright as the old light that they remember.

The former Globe Cinema at Park Hall Camp, near Oswestry, in a derelict state on March 4, 1978.

The old Shifnal railway bridge is taken down in 1953. The loss of the aesthetically pleasing old bridge and its replacement with a less elegant bridge still rankles with older Shifnal folk. Residents say that, allegedly unsafe, the cast iron bridge was supposed to have been dismantled in a weekend, but was so strongly built that it took a fortnight. *Picture: Mike Hayward.*

Birch Row, Pontesbury, in 1958, just before the demolition men got to work. It was demolished in the full knowledge of it being an important 14th-century cruck-built cottage. It was said to be the last surviving example of its type in England, and originally comprised a great central hall with tremendous oak arches, and warmed by a central hearth. Later it was subdivided and the thatch which once covered the roof was removed and replaced by galvanised sheeting. It was knocked down because it was too much bother to do it up. That's how easily history disappears. *Picture: S.R. Turner.*

Headmistress Miss Joyce Evans supervises playtime at Shelve Primary School on the last day before the closure of the school in July 1969. The 130-year-old school closed on July 18 and managers, parents, friends and pupils gathered at the school to present parting gifts. Shelve School was not actually in Shelve, but alongside the A488, between Minsterley and Bishop's Castle. Afterwards the building is thought to have been used as a youth club, a polling station, and for occasional bingo, before falling derelict. Since the mid-1980s it has been refurbished as the hub of a caravan park.

Astley Abbotts School, near Bridgnorth, was about to close when this photograph was taken in July 1962, because so few children lived in the area. Most of the children were to move to St Leonard's School, Bridgnorth.

Park Hall Camp, near Oswestry, was a major military centre over several generations. It is seen here in March 1973. By the end of the decade the site was no more than a memory and in January 1980 work was under way to reclaim the 230-acre site for agriculture and recreational uses under a £670,000 reclamation scheme.

One of the reasons why the Severn Valley Railway, a steam railway run by enthusiasts, is unlikely to be revived between Bridgnorth and Ironbridge. Here, on April 9, 1967, demolition men knock down the railway bridge between Bridgnorth Station and the railway tunnel which runs underneath the town. The bridge had been a hazard for many years and had not been used since the closure of the Severn Valley line in 1963. The enthusiasts revived the SVR south of Bridgnorth. There has been talk of late about reviving the line northwards. But the absence of this bridge is a major obstacle to that dream.

In June 1966 pupils of Ellesmere Secondary Modern School were excavating the 14th-century Myddle Castle. From left, John Butler, 14, Graham Platt, 15, and 14-year-old Robert Downs dig around the single remaining tower. Part of the tower fell in an earthquake in 1688. The rest collapsed during a gale in the late 1970s and very little now remains.

Shifnal Toll House stood on the corner of Park Lane, on the right, and the Wolverhampton road, to the left. This view of it dates from around 1931 or 1932. Behind the toll house was a garage. At some stage a lorry smashed in to the building and as a direct, or indirect, consequence, the toll house was demolished. One book asserts this happened during World War Two, but it appears to have been rather later than that. The dog running across the Wolverhampton road is an alsatian called Rascal, who lived nearby. *Picture: Joyce Danks.*

The Squirrel pub in Pound Street, Bridgnorth, around August 1971. A listed building, it opened as a pub in 1828, and closed in December 1968. At the time this photograph was taken its future was up in the air. It was hoped it would be turned into one of the town's plushest, newest, hotels. Nothing came of that idea, nor of later proposals to turn it into old people's flats. A derelict eyesore, permission was given to knock it down and build flats on the site. The building was demolished in February 1979. The new homes development built on the site is called Squirrel Court.

In December 1964 the Butchers Arms in Willow
Street, Oswestry, had lost its neighbour, and the
pub, which is thought to date back to Elizabethan
times, was itself in danger of being knocked down
and replaced by a modern building. Thankfully, it
survived. And what has gone in the site next door?
A car dealership.

A demolition gang starts work on the derelict
Methodist Church at Broseley. Of course, we're in
the sixties again. Specifically, it's November 1967.

Goodbye to the Plaza ballroom in Oswestry on January 13, 1975. It was hovering between life and death as demolition was temporary halted because the remaining part of the building was unsafe. Only the front wall facing Oswald Road remained, supported by one partially demolished side wall. There had been plans to keep the Plaza as a recreation centre, but they fell through because it would have cost too much to satisfy fire regulations. A shop now stands on the site.

During the war, Italian prisoners created their own church in a hut at their POW camp at Sheriffhales. One of them, who was clearly a talented artist, painted this fresco in the hut and proudly signed his name at the bottom: "V. DiChirico, I.P.O.W. Camp 71, 1944." By the early 1970s the hut had become dilapidated and was doomed to demolition. Here, on July 26, 1972, farm worker Eric Orwell admires the artwork. Although the makeshift church was indeed demolished soon after, the paintings were rescued thanks to a local history society and the farmer, Mr Geoffrey Johnson, of Lynbrooke. Mr Johnson had kept poultry in other huts but, out of respect for the church, did not like to put chickens in that particular hut and instead stored various things in it. The paintings were carefully removed before demolition and it was felt the best custodian for the panels was the Roman Catholic Church at Newport. Unless things have changed in the last year or so, they still exist and are in storage on the top floor of Salters Hall, the Roman Catholic priest's house in Newport, where it seems they are destined to stay until a suitable place to display them becomes available.

Bridgnorth's Crown Hotel on August 17, 1967. Woolworth's plans to adapt the Crown Hotel in the High Street as a new store created controversy in the 1960s. Woolworth's was next door, just visible to the left, and wanted to expand into the hotel building. Eventually the scheme got the go-ahead and the Crown became the new store in a tasteful conversion which retained much of the facade. The Crown pub, on the right, survives to

Demolition of the Weobley railway bridge on the A442 Wellington to Hodnet road in 1980. The bridge had crossed the old Wellington to Market Drayton railway line. The demolition was part of a £90,000 Shropshire County Council road improvement scheme.

The lamps were going out all over Ifton back in November 1968. Head lampman Mr Harry Roberts is here checking the now unused lamps at the Ifton pit, St Martins, after the announcement that it was closing. The original caption to this photo, which was taken on November 25, was: "It will be 20 weeks before the 'grand old lady of St Martins' – Ifton pit – is finally laid to rest. The pit died on Friday – axed by the National Coal Board – but today work began on the final task of stripping it of all its worldly goods, £220,000 worth of machinery… A shift of 120 men went down the pit today to start on the early salvage work."

Charles II stopped at Hubball Grange, near Tong, on his famous flight after defeat at the Battle of Worcester in 1651. By December 1966, Hubball Grange was a ruin. And, with conservation not high on the priorities in the swinging sixties, that could only mean one thing. Hubball Grange was knocked down.

Malinslee Hall on or about August 10, 1962. It already has an air of neglect and was not to last much longer. It was destroyed during the development of Telford town centre. The exact site is under Woodhouse Central, one of the inner ring roads of the centre, not far from today's Telford multiplex cinema. Scores of homes in the Malinslee and Dark Lane areas were demolished during the creation of the modern shopping centre, which opened in October 1973. There was surprisingly little protest, probably because most of the homes were old-fashioned terraced houses which were not up to modern standards. Malinslee Hall was originally built as the home of the Botfield family, who were local industrialists.

Dark Lane in February or March 1969, looking towards Top Farm in the distance. All the buildings on this picture have disappeared. This view is from what is today the Hollinswood housing estate. The area upper left is covered by the Matheson House offices, and Top Farm lies partly under the northern corner of the offices.

Ditton Priors railway station. The date is uncertain, but we guess it's the 1920s or 1930s.

Previous page: The ferry over the River Severn at Potters Loade, Highley, in February 1939. It connected Highley and Alveley, but at the time of this picture was expected to close "soon". In fact it was not closed until shortly after the war. The last ferryman was Joe Knowles, who worked the ferry from 1928 to 1947. In March 2000 his family gathered near the banks of the River Severn for a ceremonial planting of a tree bearing a plaque in his honour. Joe had lived at a ferryman's cottage only about 100 yards away from the crossing point.

How Ditton Priors station looked on May 19, 1966. It was then a ghost line. The line linking the former Royal Naval Armament Depot at Ditton Priors with the disused station was up for sale by tender in one lot. It comprised nearly 2,000 tons of line, 25,000 sleepers, and 240 telephone poles.

A goods train at Walcot railway station in the sixties.

RAF Cosford Hospital from the air in June 1977. It was opened in 1940 with 503 beds as a military hospital serving RAF Cosford. However, in the post-war period it treated many civilian patients from East Shropshire, filling a void in the health service. There were protests when it became clear it was in line for the axe, but to no avail, and it closed on December 31, 1977, just a month after the Royal Salop Infirmary in Shrewsbury closed. On the plus side, the new Copthorne Hospital, or Royal Shrewsbury Hospital as it became, was by then operational. The wartime huts at Cosford which had performed such valuable service were swept away.

The old railway station at Market Drayton is forlorn and unloved in this picture from January 1970. Market Drayton Rural District Council was to acquire the station buildings to turn them into a depot.

Lift-off! The spiked dome which for 75 years had covered the tower at Market Drayton Town Hall was safely taken down on February 21, 1972, as part of the demolition work on the town hall, which was being replaced by a new magistrates court, library, and health centre. The dome weighed about two tons and was made of lead.

A few days later it was almost all over. A demolition machine controlled by Mr Vin Huxley, of Prees, applies the "finishing touches" as Market Drayton Town Hall bites the dust.

Market Drayton Rural District Council had dismantled 10 hand pumps from council houses which were by now on mains supplies in early 1973. The pumps, many more than 50 years old, were now up for sale and were being kept in order by Mr Derek Tomkiss, a council plumber.

A great place to shop? By way of explanation, the photographer is standing in what is today's Telford shopping centre on August 15, 1962. The ruins of the Norman chapel at Malinslee are in the foreground, and Malinslee Hall is in the distance. Legend had it that there was a secret passage connecting the two. Not much is known about the history of the chapel – "obscure" is a word which often crops up in reference works. It stood roughly in the area of today's Marks and Spencer store in Telford. Telford Development Corporation went to some lengths to preserve the ruins, which were dismantled and re-erected a few hundred yards away at Telford town park, where they remain an interesting feature.

Morda House, near Oswestry, in April 1970. Morda House was opened in 1792 as a communal workhouse for the area and in its heyday housed 700 occupants. Salop County Council took it over in 1930 and it was to become a welfare home for the elderly. A landmark building, it was put on the market in 1974 and when there were no takers an application was made to have it demolished, but this was refused. Sadly Morda House was about to enjoy a new lease of life, being converted into flats, when it was hit by a fire started by arsonists in February 1982. The wrecked building was demolished the following December.

The RAF's last piston Provost trainer about to take off with Wing Commander P.A. Gifkins at the controls. It was flown from RAF Shawbury to RAF Halton in October 1969. Saying goodbye to the Provost, which was replaced by a jet version, is Pilot Officer A.E. Boxall Hunt (left) and Flight Lieutenant P.F. Finch. This particular Provost had flown a total of 2,438 hours.

Mr and Mrs Harold Burton had been running the YMCA canteen at RAF Shawbury but, in this picture from April 1968, were just about to retire. The canteen was to close. It was one of the last at an RAF camp to close in the Midlands.

What a sad and haunted scene this is! Market Drayton Rural District Council had asked Salop County Council to demolish the old railway station building at Tern Hill. The station had been acquired by the county council but – according to the rural council – it was in a dilapidated condition.

The Vine Hotel at Newport in March 1966, just before the demolition men got to work. Although the balcony was tiny, locals can remember events in which the town band squeezed on to play to the crowds below. A couple of years after this picture was taken the New Vine restaurant and balcony suite were ready on the site. By the time of its demolition the Vine Hotel was a white elephant, but Newport residents were soon to regret its passing and replacement with the new building which sits in jarringly with the street scene. That new building is a nightspot which has gone through several name changes.

SHROPSHIRE AT WAR

NO, the war didn't pass Shropshire by. Several towns were actually bombed, causing death and injuries. Bridgnorth still has a bomb site today, a gaping hole in a town centre street which has been turned into a memorial garden.

For a time during the Blitz, front-line squadrons operated from airfields carved in the north of the county. They were to score a number of "kills" as they intercepted German bombers raiding the industrial centres of the north.

For the rest of the conflict, the airfields trained fighter and bomber pilots. Even the Americans were here, at Atcham, in their P47s.

Shrewsbury is, of course, a garrison town. At Donnington, the massive Central Ordnance Depot was established by the Army at the start of the war – it was realised the depot at Woolwich was vulnerable – and was an important cog in the war effort. It led directly to the creation of a new community to house the thousands of workers. It was called New Donnington.

There were huge ammunition depots at Nesscliffe and Ditton Priors. A big Army camp at Park Hall. Various prisoner-of-war camps scattered around. Shropshire's heavy industries worked full tilt to provide the materials and arms which would lead to victory.

The Home Guard was much in evidence, on exercise or on guard duty at vital points. The Land Army worked the farms. The list goes on.

Suffice to say, it was a people's war, and Salopians played their full part.

Mrs Doris Martin, in the centre of this photograph, is seen serving in the Wenlock Civil Defence Services canteen at Coalbrookdale in 1941. The woman on the right is unknown. The woman on the left, behind the counter, is Mrs Simes of the Valley Hotel, Coalbrookdale. The picture was submitted by Mrs Martin's daughter, Mrs Mary Houlston, of Bayston Hill, Shrewsbury.

Boy Scouts help the sandbagging of Wellington Police Station on the eve of war. This photograph appeared in the old *Wellington Journal and Shrewsbury News* of September 9, 1939, but Roy "Chic" Harrison, one of the scouts involved, thinks it was taken during the school holiday in August. He is the 15-year-old scout handing up one of the sandbags to fellow scout Dennis Treherne, who is on top of the sandbags. In those days the police station was on the corner of Church Street and Plough Road. Supervising the work, second from left, is Constable Stan Thomas. The others on the photograph are not identified with any certainty – the person in the panama hat may be a Mr Nicklin and the two men at work may be council workmen. *Picture: Gwen Edwards.*

American troops marching down Broseley High Street. The date and the occasion are unknown, but presumably this is during the later years of World War Two. Picture provided by Michael and Gill Pope of Broseley Local History Society.

Auxiliary Territorial Service girl Miss Mary Collins – now Mrs Mary Brown – on a Lister truck being filled with petrol by another ATS girl at COD Donnington in 1942 or 1943. The vehicle was used to move stores around the giant depot. Although the Luftwaffe knew about the existence of Central Ordnance Depot Donnington and had taken aerial pictures of it, it was never bombed. However, it was hit by a severe fire on January 9, 1943, which burned down Shed One – the gun shed. An electrical fault was the suspected cause. *Picture: Mary Brown.*

RAF Hodnet was one of a number of small "secret" airfields in the Shropshire countryside where scores of aircraft from the crowded main air bases were flown to be stored in heavily disguised sites. So this photograph of the staff of RAF Hodnet in September 1941, posing in front of a Lockheed Hudson bomber, is extremely rare. The photograph was probably taken in the grounds of Hodnet Hall, where the aircraft were hidden among the trees. The hangars on the airfield – which was on the other side of the Shrewsbury road – were disguised as shops. Back, from left: Aircraftsman Hill, AC Moncrieff, Leading Aircraftsman Moon, AC Henderson, AC Corp, AC Manning, AC Edwards, AC Dewe, AC Hammond, LAC Cuss, AC Iles, AC Kemish, AC Robinson, AC Styles, LAC Andrews, AC Chambers. Centre row: AC Rhodes, AC Doyle, LAC Dowd, AC Springett, AC Hannah, AC Blevnev, LAC Newcombe, LAC John, AC Tedder, AC Tomlin, AC Tankard, AC Waltham, AC Evans. Front: AC Ward, LAC Smith, Corporal Clare, Cpl Bottomley, Flt Sgt Jennings, Flying Officer G.J. Pearn (Officer Commanding), Sgt Henderson, Cpl Williams, Cpl Arthur Braithwaite (from Hodnet, who had this picture hanging on his wall for years), another Cpl Williams, and AC Flux.

The visit of King George VI and Queen Elizabeth to COD Donnington on July 16, 1942. The officer in the foreground, right, is Brigadier C.E. de Wolff, the first commandant of COD Donnington, who was apparently nicknamed "Wolfy". He was deaf in one ear – and we can speculate that this was a result of combat in World War One – and wore a hearing aid which he carried under his arm. This royal visit may have been hush-hush as it seems not to have been reported by the local press. *Picture: C.O.D. Donnington.*

Digging for victory in The Quarry, Shrewsbury. It's November 1940. From left: George Salter, Bill Shipton, Cecil Smith (also known as Smudge Smith), Parks Superintendent George Ingle, and Jack James. The picture was loaned to the *Shropshire Star* by Cecil's widow, Mrs Olwyn Smith, of Shawbirch.

Staff outside the Old Rectory at Whitchurch, which played an important role in the cracking of German wartime codes. It was a top secret Y station – an eavesdropping station – which passed on intercepted coded messages to "Station X" at Bletchley Park, for decoding. This is the watch of Miss Betty Morris, later Mrs Betty Hayes, at the rectory in 1944. She is seated, middle row, third from right. Next to her, fourth from right, is Gwyneth Roberts of Shrewsbury (later Mrs Hoadley). *Picture: Betty Hayes.*

Land Army girls on the steps of Shrewsbury Castle, ready to "do their bit" while the men were away fighting.

Oops. "First crash at Shawbury aerodrome. An Avro across a road." This picture came from the album of Harry C. Harvey, an Australian airman who served at RAF Shawbury in World War One. The album was presented to RAF Shawbury by Harry's granddaughter, Mrs Jane Johnson of West Australia, on a holiday in England in 1998. Among the other pictures in the album was a photograph of the Stinchcombe sisters of Wem, and, as so often, one thing led to another, resulting in a descendant of the Stinchcombes coming over from America in 1999 to have a look at the album.

"Instructors table, Officers Mess" – a picture taken at the Atcham air base, near Shrewsbury, perhaps around 1944. During the second part of the war the base was a centre for training American fighter pilots. This picture is from the collection of the station commander, Major Ervin Miller, who says the girls were from the American Red Cross. Incidentally, it was at Atcham airfield during wartime – and quite likely in this very room – that Raymond Baxter, who is perhaps most famous for his days presenting Tomorrow's World on television, first met the young American who was to become his bride. He was at the time an instructor on Spitfires at nearby RAF Montford Bridge and went to the American base for a party. As he and his RAF colleagues, wearing their best uniform, entered the doors – possibly the doors at the end of the Nissen hut in this picture – a well-aimed ice cream came flying in their direction, which they deftly avoided. By the bar, Flying Officer Baxter saw a beautiful American girl in a green dress. She was Lieutenant Sylvia Kathryn Johnson of the US Army Nursing Corps. Their romance began that evening in the spring of 1944.

P47 Thunderbolt fighters being maintained at Atcham airfield during the war. *Picture: Major Ervin Miller.*

The Shropshire Home Guard. This picture of a military parade by the county's very own "Dad's Army" – marching past, we think, The Porthill Bridge in The Quarry, Shrewsbury – was sent in by Carole Bland-Brook. Her late father, Laurie Bland, of Wilcot House, Nesscliffe, is second from the front of the parade. We think the year is 1945.

Now, this is some line-up. It's the Home Guard pictured at the Sentinel Works, on Whitchurch Road, Shrewsbury. It's undated, but clearly it must be during the war years. This is S Company of Shrewsbury Home Guard. The picture was loaned by Mr Ivor Garbett, now of Shawbury, who worked at the Sentinel Works. Note the camouflage netting outside the works.

A Salvation Army mobile canteen serves Army patients outside Leighton Hall, between Buildwas and Shrewsbury, in about 1944. The hall was used as a Red Cross auxiliary hospital during the war. *Picture: Freda Gibbs.*

C Company, 6th Battalion, Shropshire Home Guard, 1944. These men were all, or mostly, workers at Ironbridge Power Station. Seated, in the peaked cap, centre, is believed to be Colonel Pinder, who lived in King Street, Broseley. Sitting next to him, in the light coat, is his daughter Vivian, a civilian secretary at the power station. Standing at the very back, sixth from right, is Mr Abraham Britton (known as Abe), of Queen Street, Broseley, who worked at the power station as a fitter. He was born in 1903 and served in the Home Guard during the war. He died in 1956 or 1957. The picture is thought to have been taken in a field near the power station – we are of course talking here about the 1930s power station, not the one built in the 1960s. *Picture: Joyce Pritchard.*

In the early hours of August 29, 1940, an overflying German bomber, which was probably tracking along the River Severn, unloaded its bombs on Bridgnorth. This picture, taken in October 1942, shows that two years later the scars were still visible of the bomb which landed in the road at the junction of Listley Street, St Mary's St, and Pound Street, blasting all the buildings around. On the left is the wreck of Mrs Payne's shop. Buildings nearby appear to have been repaired. The photographer has his back to the Squirrel Hotel, the front of which was blown out. Two visitors there had a narrow escape. Elsewhere in the town two people were killed by this Bridgnorth Blitz. A cottage in Church Street destroyed by one of the bombs was never rebuilt, and the bomb site is now a memorial garden. *Picture: Bridgnorth Museum.*

The Rhythm Rangers were a group which played all over Shropshire before, during, and after World War Two. They mostly comprised workers from the Sentinel Works, Shrewsbury. From left: Ivor Garbett, Phil Deacon, Alan Evans, Sid Wilkinson, Ivor's brother Ray Garbett, Ralph Sumner, Ding Broome – the one-off guest singer – Charlie Parry, and Phil Davies. *Picture: Ivor Garbett.*

Claremont Hill, Shrewsbury, looking towards the Victorian market hall in the spring of 1944. The photographer was to die within a few months of this picture being taken. His caption was "An English street with two kids that asked for 'gum.'" He was Warren R. "Russell" Lobdell, an American fighter pilot who was training on P47 Thunderbolts at nearby Atcham airfield at the time. He later moved on to operational flying and was killed in action on June 27, 1944. *Picture: Greg Hackenberg.*

Homecoming for a hero. Sergeant Harold Whitfield is feted on his return to Oswestry. He served in the King's Shropshire Light Infantry and won the Victoria Cross in 1918 – the only soldier from a Shropshire regiment to do so. Sergeant Whitfield, of Pool Farm, Middleton, near Oswestry, won the VC for capturing an enemy machine gun post single-handed in Palestine. The Victoria Cross itself has also had its adventures. The family put it into a bank at Oswestry for safe keeping. But in 1977 a 21-year-old bank clerk stole it from the vaults and sold it to a London dealer for £2,000. The dealer became suspicious, the family got the medal back, and the bank clerk got 200 hours community service. The circumstances of Whitfield's death at the age of 71 are intensely ironic. Having survived whatever the enemy could throw at him, he was knocked off his bike by an Army Land Rover while cycling home from work in 1956. The man on the right of the picture with a cap is Constable William Tench, a policeman who was controlling the crowds. *Picture: David Tench.*

This is Whitchurch High Street and this time we're in the era of World War One. Scottish troops are on church parade in the town in 1915. The picture is from a postcard franked July 17, 1915, and posted to Miss F. Smith, of Whitelands Cottage, Chelsea. The message on the back reads: "This is our high street on Sunday morning. The Scotchies on church parade." The writer was "Catherine". The sign halfway up the shop on the right is for Leonard Lee, Chemist Etc. *Picture: Ray Farlow.*

Within days of the start of World War One a large tented Army camp grew up in fields on the outskirts of Oswestry, by Gobowen Road. A photographer set up a camera on Shelf Bank, pointed it over the roofs of the Cambrian Railways Works, and took a picture which was then sent home by the soldiers as a souvenir. This particular postcard was posted to an address in South Wales and carries the message on the back: "You can see the mark on the tent where we are stopping." Close examination shows that there is an ink blob by one of the small tents on the far left. The postcard caption is "Welsh Border Infantry Brigade Camp, Oswestry, 1914" and the photographer is "F.G. Strawson, Trawsfynydd." It seems likely that there is a family connection with Miss Madge Strawson, a photographer from Bishop's Castle, who took pictures at Army camps around this time. She was the daughter of Bishop's Castle chemist George Strawson. Reporting the camp, the *Border Advertiser* of August 26, 1914, said that there was "a sea of tents… in the fields adjoining the Agricultural Show grounds and stretching for a considerable distance along under the Oswestry Coppice." On September 2 the paper reported "vanished is the great sea of tents, which sprang up in a night, and as quickly disappeared." Housing now covers the site. *Picture: Ray Farlow.*

The King's Shropshire Light Infantry C Company Bog Mines platoon during World War One, at The Bog, near Minsterley. The buildings in the background belonged to the mines and are all now demolished. Soldiers on this photograph include Lt A.E. Thomas, 2nd Lt E.C. Gray, Sgt A. France, and Sgt F.W. White. *Picture: Vera Evans.*

Carline Fields, Shrewsbury, in, we think, 1945. It's very likely that this was a VE Day celebration for the community. The picture comes from Mrs Beryl Lewis, née Lovegrove, who lived in one of the houses on the left. Born in 1931, she is the girl immediately behind the boy with his hand in his pocket on the right end of the table. The houses in this picture have long since been demolished.

Soldiers of the 1st Battalion King's Shropshire Light Infantry walking down the Liverpool landing stage to embark on the Empire Halladale, which sailed from the port in May 1955, bound for Kenya. The troops were being sent to combat the Mau-Mau rebellion. The battalion commander, Lt Col Cuthbert Brooke-Smith, was to die during the campaign in tragic circumstances. He decided to visit some "A" Company ambush positions and joined a party led by two African trackers. Unfortunately the ambush party mistook them for terrorists and opened fire. Thirty-nine-year-old Lt Col Brooke-Smith, who was from Mynd House, Little Stretton, and was known as Cuth to fellow officers, was killed. He is buried in City Park cemetery, Nairobi. His name was added to the war memorial at Church Stretton as recently as 1998. *Picture: Liverpool Post.*

CHANGING TIMES, CHANGING TOWNS

IT REALLY is only with the benefit of hindsight that we fully appreciate exactly what has vanished from our world. Or as Joni Mitchell would put it: You dunno whatcha got 'til it's gone.

The classic is of course those wide open fields to which grandmas and granddads so often refer with a wistful expression on their faces. 'Ah, yes,' they will say, longingly. 'When we were kids all this was just fields.'

And that is a sentiment expressed right across the country, because goodness knows how many acres of land have disappeared under concrete and tarmac over the past few decades.

Where children once picked wild flowers for their mums or enjoyed seemingly endless games across meadows and through woods, there now stands a housing estate… semi-detached suburbia with its neat front lawns, its patios and barbecues.

And so, yes, this section has pictures of long-gone fields, but it also has images reflecting very different changes, from a new screen being erected at the Granada cinema in Shrewsbury (it's long since been a bingo hall of course), to the old bus station and car park in Lower Barker Street.

You'll find here also the Old Market Hall at Ellesmere, Much Wenlock railway station, Bridgnorth's Low Town, a new hospital being built in Ludlow, Oswestry open market, the square at Market Drayton, and Newport Town Hall.

As The Beatles put it:
There are places I'll remember all my life,
though some have changed,
some forever, not for better,
some have gone and some remain.
All these places had their moments,
with lovers and friends I still can recall,
some are dead and some are living.
In my life I've loved them all.

Albert Gadsby's shop in Ironbridge is on the left of this view, which dates from the late 19th century. Albert himself is second left. The building was demolished around the early 1970s to make way for a mini roundabout at the bottom of Madeley Bank. Next along is the Railway Tavern, which was also demolished. The buildings on the right still stand, however. *Picture: Elaine Rye.*

Wet Wenlock. Townsfolk take cover on a rainy day in Much Wenlock. But the weather hasn't stopped two men who are up to something on the church tower. Although this photograph is undated, it can be no later than August 1930, because it was then that the church spire was taken down. It is possible this picture captures steeplejacks just about to start the work. The removal of the spire was witnessed by Jack Owen of Broseley, who was just 15 at the time and was working at Hunters tea stores in Much Wenlock High Street, delivering groceries on a carrier bike. It was his first regular job. He recalls seeing the steeplejacks putting their ladders up the steeple and fastening the rope with a cradle on. "If I remember rightly there were three of them. They were kicking their feet against the lower part of the steeple and swinging around. The people watched their antics in amazement. First of all they had to take the lead sheeting off the spire. The weight of the lead was causing the tower base to sink in to the ground."

A panorama of Much Wenlock in July 1950, with the railway in the foreground. The last passenger train from Much Wenlock to Wellington was the 7.05pm on July 21, 1962, and goods services were withdrawn on December 2, 1963. The line was officially closed on January 19, 1964. The long terraced building front right is Mardol Terrace, which dates from 1870. Inevitably, there is these days housing covering the field in the foreground. *Picture: M.E. Vere Robbins.*

Lower Barker Street and Bridge Street, Shrewsbury. This scene from the early 1950s was taken from Rowley's House following slum clearance and the creation of the bus station and car park. Cock's tannery is on the left. *Picture: S.R. Turner.*

A scene looking towards Shrewsbury from Mount Pleasant in 1949. "The spires of Shrewsbury can be seen framed between Wenlock Edge and the Stretton Hills to their left and the Long Mynd range to their right," writes Stan Turner who took the photograph. The old river bed is to the right of the picture. The field in the foreground is today part of the Mount Pleasant housing estate.

It's 1958 and the old river bed at Shrewsbury is again pictured here by photographer Stan Turner. Stan would have been surveying the scene from Cross Hill, Ellesmere Road, Shrewsbury. He says: "I took this photograph as the rising flood waters were starting to back up in the old bed. The view is looking east towards the Shrewsbury-Crewe railway line (note the steam train) and the distant Maltings. The field (top left) is now a part of the Mount Pleasant estate, and Hubert Way now runs along the right side. The Bagley Brook rises in this section of the old bed which is now a local nature reserve."

Shifnal centre in 1965. The building on the right is the Stationmaster's House, which was demolished not long after this picture was taken, as were the buildings visible beyond the Player's sign towards the left. *Picture: Mike Hayward.*

Some Market Drayton folk were thinking – when this picture was taken back in June 1956 – that the old Buttercross should be pulled down. Others heatedly disagreed. So, said the newspaper of the day, the council was to adjudicate that week. Now then, if we either (a) go to Market Drayton, or (b) consult Michael Raven's excellent, breathtakingly detailed Shropshire Gazetteer (1989), we find the happy ending to this story. Raven tells us: "In Cheshire Street we find the Buttercross, a small open-sided market hall of 1834 with Tuscan columns and a pediment. On top is a small bellcote with two fire bells."

This is what it used to be like when you went to the post office. This is Dawley sub post office in October 1961.

In characteristic pose at the top of Cartway, Bridgnorth, in August 1960, is John Sherry, relaxing on the doorstep of his home with what looks like a pint in his hand. His cat Tiddles is nowhere to be seen – perhaps Tiddles saw the dog approaching and ran off. Further down the street you get a glimpse of the Black Boy Inn, which retains that name today.

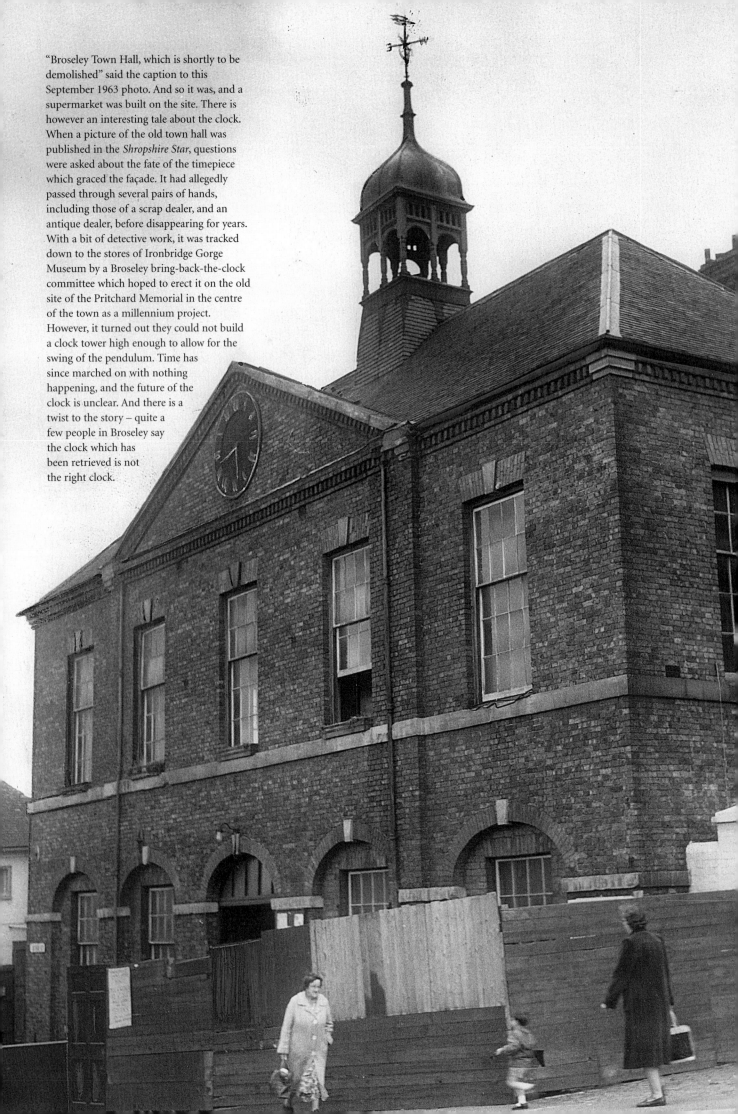

"Broseley Town Hall, which is shortly to be demolished" said the caption to this September 1963 photo. And so it was, and a supermarket was built on the site. There is however an interesting tale about the clock. When a picture of the old town hall was published in the *Shropshire Star*, questions were asked about the fate of the timepiece which graced the façade. It had allegedly passed through several pairs of hands, including those of a scrap dealer, and an antique dealer, before disappearing for years. With a bit of detective work, it was tracked down to the stores of Ironbridge Gorge Museum by a Broseley bring-back-the-clock committee which hoped to erect it on the old site of the Pritchard Memorial in the centre of the town as a millennium project. However, it turned out they could not build a clock tower high enough to allow for the swing of the pendulum. Time has since marched on with nothing happening, and the future of the clock is unclear. And there is a twist to the story – quite a few people in Broseley say the clock which has been retrieved is not the right clock.

Although England's parish churches are renowned as symbols of continuity, there have been quite a few changes to this Broseley scene which, although undated, seems from the evidence of the car to be from the late 1930s. The car, we think, is an Austin Eight or something called an Austin Big Seven. Today the yew tree visible through the gates has disappeared, together with the gravestones in the churchyard. The pinnacles on the church tower were removed for safety reasons in about 1950. The lights on top of the gates appear somewhat shrunken today. All Saints Church at Broseley is comparatively new, dating from 1845 and built at a cost of a little over £9,000, but there have been at least two previous churches on the site. The churchyard is now 'closed', which means nobody is buried there now.

Broseley again, and a building which had a narrow escape. In the mid-1960s developers envisaged an ultra-modern town centre, including a civic centre. Victoria Hall, seen here on March 18, 1965, would have been knocked down to make way for it all. The plans never reached fruition. Although Broseley has not completely been spared modern buildings on the High Street, it has by and large dodged the worst excesses and still retains its traditional feel. Indeed, its centre is a designated Conservation Area.

Work proceeding on the new magistrates court, library and health centre buildings in Cheshire Street, Market Drayton. We don't have the exact date, but it is likely to be late 1972 or maybe early 1973.

The original caption of this picture was: "A general view of the first sale at Shrewsbury's new attested market on Tuesday. Earl St Aldwyn (Parl. Sec. to Min of Ag) assisted by Alderman H.O. Ashton (managing director of a local firm of auctioneers) sells the first animal." The date was July 17, 1956. The champion cow belonged to Mr B.J. Whittingham senior, of Bomere Heath, who is standing in the corner behind the cow, which sold for £115.

Ah! The magic of the silver screen. A brand new screen is installed at The Granada cinema, Shrewsbury, in September 1967. This magnificent 1930s picture house and theatre was eventually converted into a bingo hall.

It took five hours for firefighters to quell the flames at the works of J.B. Joyce and Co. in Station Road, Whitchurch, in November 1964. However, despite the damage, production of clocks at the famous clock firm was not affected. Clocks made by the firm have been used across the world, including by municipal buildings in Cape Town, the Sydney Post Office, and the Customs House in Shanghai. Here a fireman is seen battling with the blaze from an extension ladder.

Whitchurch High Street on October 5, 1966. On the left is Whitchurch Town Hall which was almost totally destroyed by fire in December 1941. It was known as the Regent Cinema and seated hundreds of people. The upper part of the building was lost and there was considerable damage to the Corn Exchange beneath. A "temporary roof" was put over the ground floor and adjacent Market Hall which was used as the main Assembly Hall for more than 25 years before the modern Whitchurch Civic Centre was built on the site, opening in 1970.

The Old Market Hall, Ellesmere, photographed in 1976.

PREFABS DOOMED wailed the headline in the *Shropshire Journal* in the story accompanying this picture, which was taken on June 7, 1967. The death sentence had been passed on the prefabs at Woodlands Avenue and Lawrence Road, Wellington, meaning 50 tenants would have to be found new homes. The bungalows had been erected by the Ministry of Works in 1947-48 to help the post-war housing crisis and their useful life was given as 10 years. However, an inspection had shown that there was corrosion of the aluminium framework and wall panels. The response of people living there to the news was mixed. "They are bitter cold in winter" said one, but others said they made comfortable homes despite their age.

And the other side of the story. These are Madeley's old prefabs in Station Road in March 1963. Unlike those at Wellington, the council decided to do them up. They survive to this day.

The original caption to this May 1962 picture was: "This is the market square at Bishop's Castle – surely the smallest? But then Bishop's Castle is the smallest borough in England, and with a population of 1,229 at the 1961 census, it is now recommended that it should be merged with the rural district at Clun." The W.H. Jarvis store no longer exists. Bill Jarvis was town mayor six times and a town councillor for 50 years. The man sitting at the bench could be his father-in-law James Evans, who used to spend hours sitting there. The building across the street with the warehouse doors belonged to Evans egg dealers and was used for storage, and between the buildings, beyond the cars, is Broads drapery store, which in more modern times has been an antiques shop. When this picture was published, an instruction was given to the newspaper artist to "take out the Park Drive sign" – to avoid giving them free advertising, one supposes. This has only been partly successful – can you spot it?

This is the sad scene at the once proud Oswestry station in March 1971 after the end of passenger services. The Shropshire town was once the biggest railway centre in the county, being the headquarters of Cambrian Railways and home of the Cambrian Railways workshops in the days of steam. Around 800 in the town looked to the railway for their employment. But death by Beeching came in the mid-1960s. Our picture shows the view looking north-east, towards the works (not visible) and where the lines to Gobowen and Whitchurch (via Ellesmere) diverged. The station building on the left still stands, adjacent to the current HQ of the Cambrian Railways preservation group which is trying to reopen the line from Gobowen to Llanyblodwel and Llanymynech, with steam haulage part of the project. But the building and canopy in the centre of the picture has been swept away, with just fragments of the old platform surviving alongside the one rusty track that passes through what was once a mighty railway town.

Another heartbreaking picture for railway enthusiasts and fans of Victorian buildings everywhere. This is the old station house at Much Wenlock. Roof tiles missing, windows boarded up, nature overwhelming the platform, and all but forgotten. The picture is from 1971.

A group of disappointed young would-be bathers stand beside the brand new swimming pool at Newport after being told they could not take the plunge yet. The baths' heating plant had not had time to warm the water. It is April 1968. With the children in this picture is Mr Eric Sorrill, chairman of the Newport and District Swimming Pool Trust. An official opening of the new pool was to take place with the chairman of Newport Urban District Council, A.W. Harding, officiating.

The Royal Oak Hotel in Cheshire Street, Market Drayton carries a "Sold" sign on its frontage. But it didn't bring with it a bright new future. We don't know when this photograph was taken, but would guess it was in 1973 or 1974, as in 1974 a whole load of buildings in Cheshire Street were demolished including, we think, the Royal Oak, as it no longer exists. The small poster in the front window appears, under magnification, to read "Vote Cassidy, vote Liberal." And you will remember there were two general elections in 1974. The Royal Oak had been built in 1871 on the site of the 17th-century Oak Inn.

Another one bites the dust. The end for Newport Railway Station in March 1968.

Mini van, Morris Minor, Morris 1100, Triumph Herald… and, oh yes, Church Stretton High Street. This picture was taken on May 5, 1967. The Raven pub closed a few years later. In front of it had stood Church Stretton's Victorian market hall, which was demolished in July 1963 because it was said to be unsafe. The site has been left open ever since.

The oldest shop in Whitchurch, retaining its original frontage and style, is Ye Olde Shoppe, a 16th-century structure, here photographed in August 1963.

Ludlow's Roman Catholic Church nears completion in Henley Road in June 1936. A bell sits by the door awaiting installation.

November 1964. Bridgnorth's Low Town as seen from the borough's other half – High Town. It's a bleak winter scene and one very familiar to many locals.

Workmen are demolishing a warehouse in St Mary's Street, Bridgnorth, in this picture from July 1970. The idea was to make an access road to a new supermarket being built in the High Street. The warehouse was used by the trustees of Charles Deighton, a wine and spirits firm, founded in the town in 1729, until it closed in the March of 1970. Workmen are pictured watching as timbers fall. Okay, so it may not look like very much of a building in this photograph, but still it's another piece of disappearing history.

October 1969 and the first £250,000 phase of rebuilding East Hamlet Hospital, Ludlow, is changing the skyline of the town. Nurse G. Lucas and Staff Nurse M. Capper are seen walking past the new geriatric ward now being built at the hospital. The new ward was to cater for 66 patients. Included in the first phase were a new boiler house and improvements to the electrical facilities of the hospital.

Hustle and bustle at Oswestry open market in February 1970.

Dawley Bank in the pre-Telford days. The date is likely to be August 1962.

Border country. The village of Llanymynech straddles the England and Wales border. The Lion Hotel used to be all in England. Then, sometime in the early 1800s or thereabouts, the frontage was built on – into Wales. The consequence is that the front of the premises is now in Wales, and the back is in England. Until the introduction of the poll tax, the Lion would pay two sets of rates – rates for Shropshire for the back rooms, and rates for Wales for the front part. However it is now, for payment purposes, deemed to be all in Shropshire, even though it isn't. A cross on the wall in the front lounge bar marks the border. The Vaggs Motors bus on the right will be in the process of turning round. This was its terminus for the journey from Shrewsbury, and it turned round here to make the return journey. The driver is probably waiting for the right time to depart. The photograph is undated but seems to be from the 1960s.

Beauty or the beast? Ludlow Town Hall divided opinions locally. One view was that it was a "monstrous sore" before which all loyal citizens averted their eyes. It is seen here in June 1958. In its last years it was increasingly unloved, and when it was declared unsafe the demolition men moved in with almost indecent haste. It was knocked down in March 1986. During the work they came across a Victorian time capsule buried under the foundation stone with a copy of the Ludlow Advertiser inside dated September 15, 1888. This was puzzling, as you can see that at the top of the building it declares it was "Erected AD 1887". The explanation may be that it was planned in 1887 and was intended to commemorate the golden jubilee of Queen Victoria. It was in fact opened on October 17, 1889, by local MP Lt Col Windsor-Clive. Whatever you may think about the old town hall, its going has left a large gap in the Ludlow Square, and the town lost a fine town council chamber and a large function room.

Ludlow bypass taking shape at Fishmore Road, Ludlow, on September 16, 1977. The road opened on February 4, 1980, taking heavy traffic out of the centre of the historic town. The route of the road is a long, wide sweep to the east of Ludlow. Some council officials openly preferred a route which would have bypassed the town to the west, which would have been much more direct, but would have seen lorries and heavy traffic thundering along at the foot of Ludlow Castle.

A refractory chimney topples to the ground during demolition at the gas works at Sherrymill Hill, Whitchurch, in April 1973.

Er, we're not quite sure what this picture is all about, apart from the fact that it is something to do with the cobbles in Broad Street, Ludlow, and was taken on March 11, 1960. The reason for our ignorance is that the original caption has been damaged. The bits we can read are this: "...to make... 'We'll camp...' said an oppo... the Rt Rev E.... of Ludlow and a... of Hereford. M... are supporting him... cries of 'vandalism'... workmen recently co... the cobbles on the e... the street." Sorry to say this, but you're going to have to work it out yourself! The cobbles in Broad Street are still there, incidentally.

A typical Shropshire street scene – The Square at Market Drayton in the sixties.

The National Provincial Bank at Market Drayton was housed in one of the town's oldest buildings, the caption to this picture informed us in September 1966. This half-timbered structure marks the line of the great fire at Market Drayton which swept through the town in 1651. The building had – in 1966 – been undergoing extensive renovations.

A view over Oswestry from the top of St Oswald's Church in September 1964. In the foreground, behind the trees, is Bellan House School. The Broad Walk in front of it, nearer the camera, has been spruced up in recent years and there is now a plaque on the wall below the trees to Wilfred Owen, the war poet, who was born in Oswestry. Note that there is some building going on in the upper left of the picture. Top right is Shelf Bank.

Newport as it was, looking towards The Wrekin in the distance. The photograph dates from on or about February 1, 1961. The two-storey building on the far right is rooms 5 and 10 of Adams' Grammar School. The building next to it, also two storeys but lower, is the new staff common room which opened in 1959. Next there is a single-storey building, which was known as the manual room – at the time woodwork was done there – and next to that is the Combined Cadet Force hut. Carrying on, at the foot of the three poplars, is the canteen. The house in the distance to the right of the poplars is Vauxhall House, with Longford Hall hidden among the trees on the skyline above. The black and white building is the Honeysuckle pub. Today, the open fields in the distance are covered with new housing.

Newport Town Hall, erected in 1860, was described as a "monstrosity" by one speaker at a local meeting in 1963. The gathering was called to ask the local urban district council to encourage traders to plan a Civic Trust scheme to brighten up the town.

It's June 14, 1974, and work on the new M54 motorway is well under way, running diagonally in the upper part of the picture. In the foreground is the A5 which it effectively bypassed. In fact, the new road was known as the Wellington bypass, and didn't really go anywhere. It opened on December 11, 1975. Later it was extended eastwards and this new section linking it to the main motorway network was opened on November 25, 1983. We are looking over Priorslee. On the right is St George's Church, which gave its name to the nearby community of St Georges which had, until a public meeting on December 19, 1859, been known as Pain's Lane.

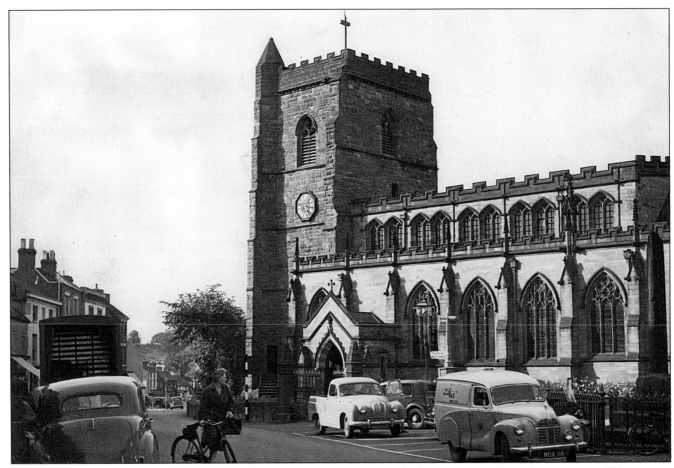

The Church of St Nicholas stands at the centre of the market town of Newport. Built of red standstone, its register dates from 1569. This photograph is from November 1954.

PROUD SALOPIANS

WHAT does it mean to be a "Salopian"? Let us quote you the views of one "incomer" Salopian, and one Shropshire-born – and leave you to make your own minds up.

According to the late Sir Julian Critchley, who was from London and came to Wistanstow, near Craven Arms, as an evacuee: "If there are distinguishing characteristics it's a sort of Anglo-Welshness. I mean there are so many Shropshire people who are called Evans, Morris, Jones, Griffiths, whatever. My mother was a Morris.

"So it's difficult to say that the Salopian is either English or Welsh. He is a cross breed, a mongrel.

"I would have thought a characteristic of the older generation of Salopians, thinking of my uncles and aunts, were that they were all a bit tight-fisted. They weren't exactly mean, but they weren't particularly generous.

"The years between the wars were so difficult for the farming communities and people who depended on the farmers' incomes like shopkeepers that they were brought up not to brake their cars sharply because it meant they wore their tyres out.

"There was a carefulness towards money that is not the case today. Before the war the Salopian was a shade dour, not given to flights of fancy, and drank quite a lot, particularly cider which was much more common in those days.

"Increasing prosperity, the telly, and travel have ironed out a lot of the differences, which is a pity, but nonetheless inevitable.

"I don't think Shropshire people are more friendly than anyone else. I think the further north you go the more friendly people are and the better the black pudding. You don't get really good black puddings until you get beyond the Chester line."

Wellington-born local historian George Evans says: "The adjective which goes with Salopian is Proud Salopian, but I'm not at all sure that isn't exclusively Shrewsbury. Shrewsbury would like to think so.

"Shropshire has an identity of sorts. It's an identity in diversity, as they say in the United States. Yes there is a Shropshire identity, in spite of the diversity of north Shropshire, south Shropshire, the Welsh border, the Wrekin, and so on.

"I think we're friendly – and are quite prepared to fight anybody who says we're not."

Hooked. Firefighters at Wem show off the large firefighters' hook which was on display in the town's fire station. It was 29ft long and was used to drag blazing thatch from houses in the town in bygone days. According to Station Officer Mick Dee it would have been used at the time of the great fire of Wem in March 1677 in which almost all the town was destroyed. At the time of this picture, which was taken in September 1976, he was looking for ways of commemorating the event, presumably to mark the 300th anniversary of the disaster.

Billy Lloyd by the Captain Webb Memorial in Dawley with a couple of young friends, perhaps in the late 1950s. "Little Billy", as he was known, was just 4ft 4ins tall and was one of the great Shropshire characters of the 20th century. He is holding the bag in which he carried the newspapers he delivered. He had a trolley with which he delivered them, which must be somewhere nearby. Older folk from Dawley remember Billy as being ever-cheerful, with an unforgettable laugh. *Picture: Freda Goucher.*

Run for cover! It's the incensed womenfolk of Stirchley on the warpath! These homeowners from Claverley Drive were unhappy when, back in September 1974, they caught wind of the fact that Wrekin Council was planning to buy 25 houses at Stirchley to rent out as council houses. The private owners were worried that the value of their own homes would fall as a result. They accused the council and the site developers, Maxwell Homes, of unfair tactics. From left: Mrs Judy Latham, Mrs Candy Tetlon, Mrs Christine Shaw, Mrs Sandra White, Mrs Diane Burns, Mrs Beryl Jones, Mrs Eva Smith, Mrs Linda Sprigings, and Mrs Catherine Duffy.

Children of Orleton Lane Infants School, Wellington, take a close look at one of the puppets after the Harlequin puppet show which was part of the Wellington Arts Festival in May 1967.

Part of the parade before, or after, the Ludlow hospital service on October 16, 1966.

Shrewsbury sales consultant Keith Wylie carried out his threat to picket his local pub in July 1967. For 30 minutes he walked up and down outside the Yorkshire House, Shrewsbury, calling on the brewery – Greenall Whitley's – to put his favourite brew back on sale. But the brewery said it was not the company's policy to sell the type of beer Mr Wylie wanted. Keith was kept going during his picket with cups of – coffee! – served to him by the bikini-wearing Rozanne Griffiths of Church Stretton.

Male nurses at Shropshire Orthopaedic Hospital are to have a whole new look, reports the November 1970 story which accompanies this picture. "Final decisions are still to be made on their new uniform. Wearing the proposed new male nurse uniform is (left) Enrolled Nurse Anthony John, watched by student nurses Stuart Westbook and Ann Lloyd."

Shropshire Star photographer John Roberts obtained special permission to take this picture and others at the Closed Order of the Convent of Poor Clares at Ellesmere in June 1974. Here the Sisters walk along the cloister singing psalms as they make their way to the dining hall.

Newport Urban District Council chairman, Councillor D.J. Green, is seen leaving the parish church after the Civic Sunday service in June 1965. In the background is Colonel E.J. Coulthard who later took the salute at the march past. The Rev John Barratt, Newport Methodist minister, also took part.

"Two proud kings of the jungle who once stood guard on the Lilleshall Monument lie dejected in a field half a mile away hoping that one day they may be reinstalled in their rightful domain. Pictured with the lions are the wife and daughter of the vicar of Lilleshall, Mrs M. Smith, and baby Sara." The picture dates from October 1966. Actually, the last word of the original caption is missing, so Sara may have had a double-barrelled first name.

Brownies leave Malinslee Church after the St George's Day service on April 20, 1968. They marched to Dawley, where Lord Bridgeman took the salute.

A parade of school uniforms at Market Drayton Secondary Modern School in February 1965. Front row (left to right): Cheryl Walker in her smart two-piece indoor uniform which had been adopted for all girls going to the new comprehensive school, and Heather Lynn and Doreen Peacock in the uniforms of the Grammar and Modern schools. The three other girls display the old and new outdoor uniforms. They are Sally Hobson (Comprehensive), Ann Reynold (Modern), and Christine Jones (Grammar).

Surrounded by beer-making equipment is Mr John Tidswell, taking time off for a cup of tea at his wine and beer-making stall at Oswestry open air market in November 1968. It all started as a hobby when John was an insurance broker. By 1968 he was making about five gallons of beer a week – but wasn't drinking it all himself!

Bert Mitchell, boss of A.R. Mitchell at 32 St John's Hill, Shrewsbury, with an EEG machine – one of the first made. These machines do scans of the brain. The firm was a pioneer in the field, making dozens of these in an attic workshop at its Shrewsbury premises from around the late 1940s into the 1950s, and the picture dates from around then. The electroencephalograph was developed by Harold Shipton of Shrewsbury and Dr Gray Walter. *Picture: David Mitchell.*

Cubs and brownies who attended the "thinking day" service at Leaton Parish Church near Shrewsbury in February 1968.

Mr Gordon N. Norris had been custodian of the clock at St Nicholas's Church, Newport, for 50 years when this picture was taken in February 1961. Every Friday he cycled to the church and then climbed up the 54 steps within the tower to the clockroom where it was his job to wind up the heavy weights that keep the mechanism ticking.

The Rev G. Thomson watches Mr Larry Mossop prepare to hoist the weathercock back up Worfield Parish Church spire in the April of 1968. The weathercock was brought down while the spire was being renovated.

It's October 1956 and the Roman Catholics of the Shrewsbury diocese celebrate the second of the services for the centenary of their cathedral on Town Walls.

Miss Fanny Jones was one of three sisters who ran a legendary tea shop at Chelmick Pools, near Church Stretton, which was a magnet for walkers and hikers in the Stretton Hills for generations. She is seen here in September 1954 walking towards her thatched cottage – the tea shop itself was a little chalet in the garden. Fanny, Sarah, and Mary Ellen lost their home in early August 1955 when a spark set fire to the thatched roof of the elderly sisters' cottage and it burnt down. And although the tea room was not affected, it spelt the end for this much-loved refreshment spot in the Chelmick valley, near Hope Bowdler, which had served up so many delicious home-made teas over the years. However there remains a link with the past through the wisteria, which survived the fire, and which still grows up the wall of the new home built on the site of the wrecked cottage.

Oyez, oyez. A town crier announces the festivities for the Oswestry charter celebrations on March 30, 1974. For 10 hours many people stood on the Bailey Head, the old market place, and were entertained by plays, music and dancing involving over 200 local people. The event was organised to celebrate the tercentenary of the granting of the town's Royal Charter by Charles II. The event culminated with a Stuart-period market.

A passing-out parade was held at the Sir John Moore Barracks, Shrewsbury, in September 1971. The passing-out platoon, Minden, is seen marching past the inspecting officer, Brigadier D.M. Pontifex.

We would love to tell you exactly what this meeting at St Mary's School in Albrighton in October 1969 is all about, but we're afraid we can't, because we don't know. It was obviously quite a high powered affair because the hall is packed and the person at the end of the table nearest the camera is Gerry Fowler, who was the local MP. Maybe people from the Albrighton area will be able to recognise some of the faces in the audience.

A dustman and a cook appear to be taking the salute at a marchpast at RAF Tern Hill on January 27, 1967. In fact, dustman Jim Broadhurst, 65, and 51-year-old cook Woolf Morris, were receiving "gongs", along with three RAF officers and a sergeant. Air Commodore F.L. Dodd presented the Air Officer Commanding's commendation to Mr Broadhurst, of Market Drayton, who had been working as a garbage collector for the station since 1951. And he presented the Air Officer Commanding In Chief's recommendation to Mr Morris, also of Market Drayton, who had been the head cook for the officers' mess at Tern Hill for 17 years.

The patron of the Shropshire British Legion, Viscount Bridgeman, takes the salute as 65 legion banners and more than 600 Shropshire members enter the grounds of Shrewsbury Castle where a special drumhead service of thanksgiving is being held. It is September 1964 and the service is to commemorate the two world wars.

Newport Congregational Chapel's harvest supper. Our print had the date October 24, 1959, stamped on the back, but that could be a reprint date as it is thought it was actually taken around 1956. Mrs Mary Connelly is in the light patterned top in the centre of the back row. Seventh from the left on the back row is Miss Sylvia Taylor, who would only have been about 14 at the time, and next along is a Mrs Amos, whose husband was a signalman at Stafford station. Fourth along to the right from Mrs Connelly, the tall gentleman, is a Mr Loveday, who worked at Serck Audco, and the man next right is Harold Davies, manager of the MEB offices in Newport. In the rear seated row, far left is Edith Henshall, known as Edie, whose husband had a cobbler's shop in Newport. And in the centre of the row with her hat nearly down to her eyes is Mrs Hurd, a widow. Then three along, in a leopard-spot top, is Mrs W. Lewis, and then Mrs Katherine Lewis who taught at Newport CofE School.

A motorist's nightmare. Oswestry's new traffic wardens were about to start their duties in October 1971, and were completing their training sessions in Shrewsbury. From left are Gordon Pryce Jones, of Oswestry, and William Camlin, of Criggion.

SCENES OF TRANQUILLITY

PICTURE the scene. It's morning and it's time to get up. Within just a few minutes one teenage son has Radio One blaring from his bedroom, another teenage son has the latest Radiohead album blasting out, competing for attention. You go downstairs and your wife has GMTV on in the lounge and, simultaneously, Radio Two on in the kitchen, while at the same time the kettle is boiling, the toaster is popping up, and the washing machine is already in a spin. Then the phone rings and someone's schoolpal is knocking at the front door.

Ever wished you could get away from it all?

How about a stroll on Wenlock Edge? How about finding a forgotten corner of Acton Burnell Castle with nothing for company but a good book and a flask of coffee?

Fancy a picnic on Lilleshall hill?

Fancy a long walk around the country lanes of Church Pulverbatch?

All these humble pursuits are hinted at in this section. And you'll also find pictures of Aston-on-Clun, Atcham, Buildwas Abbey, and the ancient Priory gatehouse at Bromfield.

There's the pretty-as-a-picture church at Astley Abbotts captured on film way back in 1935. From around the same time, there's a photograph of Morville Church.

There's the trickling River Onny at Onibury and there's the Moat House at Orleton Hall in Wellington. There's the River Severn at Quatford and there's the much-loved Umbrella House on the old A5 near Wellington too.

Here we have those quiet backwaters for which Shropshire is justly famous.

Feeling stressed? This could be the section for you!

A view from Wenlock Edge. The year is 1939. However, things are not quite what they seem! Because this is a clever cut and paste job. The woman and the rock she is standing on have been cut out and stuck on to the print of the panoramic scene.

Rowton Castle, "before the fire", according to the original caption. The print carried the datestamp of March 5, 1953. As this was actually the date of the fire, it is obviously an older picture which was dragged out from the archives to print at the time of the blaze. The fire was especially serious because the castle and its grounds were the home at the time for students attending the unusually-named Royal Normal College for the Blind. It broke out in the early hours, completely destroying the sleeping accommodation for about 50 blind students in single-storeyed dormitories in the grounds of the castle. It also destroyed the music and tuning room, together with about 34 pianos, including a number of grand pianos and three organs including an electronic organ. The fire spread from these timber buildings down a corridor to a two-storey building in which were housed about another 50 blind students. This building was also damaged. But none of the students were hurt and all were evacuated to the castle building itself without mishap.

Cleobury Mortimer's twisted church spire is seen to good effect in this 1962 picture taken from the meadows behind the town.

Ever popular with visitors to Acton Burnell is the 13th-century castle. It is certainly an attraction for little boys as this picture from 1962 testifies.

A time-honoured discussion among fishermen about the ones that got away, seen in the yard of the Mytton and Mermaid, Atcham, on August 25, 1953. The fishermen were founder members of the Express and Star Angling Club who were having a lunchtime chat and drink at their favourite Shropshire hotel. On the left is Geoff Mason, then comes chief photographer George Pringle and, on the right, George Rowley. The person who took this photograph was Peter Garland. The Mytton and Mermaid was the club's regular haunt. Members used to borrow the chairman's shooting brake on a Sunday, have four or five hours good fishing, a couple of beers and then a chat.

A popular Shropshire viewpoint on a summer's day is Lilleshall Hill, from which this view of The Wrekin can be enjoyed. The photograph is from August 1953.

The ferry at Hampton Loade on August 23, 1954. The ferry normally crossed the River Severn five feet below this level – the river was running higher than usual when this picture was taken. The ferryman is Mr W.J. Parkes, of Ferry House, Hampton Loade, who had been taking passengers across the river for 12 years. There have been various twists and turns in the fortunes of the ferry. The lowest moment was in December 1964 when it was swept away in floods and the 22-year-old ferry operator was killed. In recent years, it sank completely in 2000, and partially in 2003. But it keeps bouncing back, the last survivor in Shropshire of this ancient way of crossing the River Severn.

A bracing winter's day in 1958 and this is the view from Cothercott Hill, near Church Pulverbatch. The rolling Shropshire plain is visible for many miles.

The freak weather has its effect on the River Roden, where it spills over at Rodington in July 1968.

This sounds just the place to be on a rainy day. The Umbrella House, near Wellington, has been a landmark on the old A5 since 1835 when its canopy-type roof gave it its name. Originally, it was the toll house.

Children walk home from school in the sunshine through the pretty hamlet of Upton Magna in October 1958. In the background is the parish church. The cottage in the background is called Porch House and is one of the Elizabethan timber framed cottages in the village. But Upton Magna's Elizabethan homes are positively modern compared to a cruck cottage in the village which has been dated to 1269, making it the oldest cottage of its type in Europe.

Ducks swim peacefully on the waters by the 16th-century water mill at Weston, near Oswestry. Behind the walls the local baker, Mr Levin Bennett, used the mill as his bakery and was still mixing the dough by water power. The photograph was taken in August 1961. The bakery tradition at the old mill has been continued by his son John, in partnership in the business with his brother Levin – named after his late father – although electricity has taken over from water power.

Stanton Mill, near Stanton-upon-Hine-Heath, is one of Shropshire's lost gems. The last miller there was Ted Lycett – "Ted The Miller". The mill appears to have stopped working in the late 1940s, although the story which accompanied this picture in late September 1962 – when Salop County Council approved demolition – quoted a councillor as saying it was working "up to five years ago". It was proposed to replace the mill with a garage for lorries. The locals weren't exactly happy. Demolition however must have gone ahead not long after this photograph was taken. All that stands there now is a galvanised steel shed.

An attractive scene as Beryl Lockett, exercising horses from Betton House, passes through the village of Betton, near Market Drayton. It is December 1972.

At a rehearsal for a forthcoming youth pilgrimage to Lichfield Cathedral, a procession passes through the grounds of Haughmond Abbey's beautiful ruins at Shrewsbury. At the abbey, the then Bishop of Shrewsbury, Rt Rev R.L. Hodson, held a service. This was July 1958.

Children in the woods at Aston-on-Clun in February 1967.

A summer scene at Atcham with cows enjoying the cool waters of the River Severn. The Mytton and Mermaid Hotel can be seen peeping between the trees in the background. This photograph – taken in 1969 – was for use in a calendar.

The custodian of Buildwas Abbey, Mr John Mills (or Jack), prepares for spring visitors in 1959. Mr Mills had been custodian since 1927.

Bromfield's Priory gatehouse is a splendid Tudor building. Its great studded doors are holed in places; probably this was done during the Civil War. For a time the place was used as the village school, and later as a recreation room. It stands on a peninsula formed by the Rivers Onny and Teme. The picture is from November 1954.

Cheswardine photographed for the old *Wellington Journal and Shrewsbury News* in November 1964.

The village church at Astley Abbotts captured on Easter Sunday 1935.

Morville Church, one of the oldest in Shropshire, stands upon a Saxon foundation. The picture is from August 1939.

It's May 1957 and the old people of Clun are photographed at the Holy Trinity Hospital.

Hermitage Farm near Hawkstone Park photographed in February 1959. The hill in the background was often used by motorcyclists for scrambling.

The North Shropshire Hounds at the Boxing Day meet at Hodnet. The year? 1965.

A car starts to descend The Burway into Church Stretton – one of Shropshire's most spectacular drives. The hill in the distance on the left is The Lawley, which was at the centre of a huge row in the 1980s when its side was turned into a massive "billboard" by a farmer to advertise his goods, by using weedkiller or similar to discolour the grass and spell out his advertising message. Although outraged local folk claimed the action had desecrated the hillside for years, in fact the wording faded out within a few weeks. In the centre is Caer Caradoc, which some think was the site of Caractacus's last stand against the Romans (Caractacus was the Roman name for Caradoc). This photograph dates from July 1956.

Two drinkers sup a pint in the courtyard of the Rose and Crown, Ludlow, in April 1960. The yard is recorded back as far as 1102, when it was part of a monastery. The first licence for the premises was granted in 1603.

Imagine how cold and windy it is for these walkers who are taking a stroll on the Long Mynd, probably in the late 1930s. The Long Mynd is such a vast expanse that in the past people have got lost, and died, there.

A scene at the village of Onibury where the placid River Onny trickles over shingled steps and lazily curls around green slopes. It is the August of 1956.

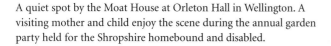

A quiet spot by the Moat House at Orleton Hall in Wellington. A visiting mother and child enjoy the scene during the annual garden party held for the Shropshire homebound and disabled.

The Three Fishes at Bayston Hill in January 1958. Host Percy Gibbons had collected more than 100 pieces of brass over a number of years, and polished them weekly. He is seen at work.

The River Severn at Quatford on a summer's day in 1939.

A Last Look

HERE we go with one last selection, giving us a chance to cram in some photos which don't sit well in the previous chapters, or pictures we just feel like squeezing in.

Call it a bonus chapter if you like.

The photos in the book have mostly covered the last 50 years or so. You've seen with your own eyes how much things have changed in that time.

But in another way, things have changed little. Shropshire still boasts some of the most beautiful scenery in Britain. Quaint villages are, by and large, still quaint. Farmers still work the countryside.

What will things be like in 50 years' time?

A recent report by the Campaign to Protect Rural England paints a grim picture. The distinctive character of the countryside and our lovely market towns is being wrecked, it says. Chain store supermarkets, miserable housing designs, and ill-conceived agricultural changes are moving the countryside towards blandness and uniformity, eroding the diversity which makes the rural landscape such a joy.

Time will tell whether the CPRE is right.

We do know, however, that Salopians will be different. Oh yes they will. Those Shropshire folk alive today who have memories, anecdotes, and insights into the scenes in this book will no longer be around to share their reminiscences with us. The passing of time destroys common knowledge and common experience.

So this book really is a last look at the life and times of previous generations, before those generations fade away and their voices are lost.

A guard of honour of prams outside the wives club at RAF Tern Hill in September 1960.

In September 1969, Wrekin MP Gerry Fowler visited the new primary school in Park Lane, Shifnal, and met its parents action committee to talk about ways to improve safety for children on their way to school. He led the committee members as they went over one of the routes the children would take.

When the Severn Valley Railway through Bridgnorth closed in September 1963, there were enthusiasts who were determined not to let the SVR die. In 1965 there was a meeting at the Coopers Arms in Kidderminster of people who wanted to save the line. Over the years they gathered locomotives and rolling stock – as demonstrated by this April 1968 picture taken at Bridgnorth Railway Station. A British Rail team about to tear up the track were halted by an 11th hour telegram. The enthusiasts got permission to run from Bridgnorth to Hampton Loade in 1970 and raised the money to buy the land. Since then, it has been a story of expansion, and the SVR is thriving.

An advanced party of American troops arrived at Ditton Priors on January 18, 1967, ready for the takeover of the former Royal Navy armaments depot. Around 250 soldiers were expected to arrive over the coming days as it became an American ammunition base. The US Army was not there long. The last of them left on July 1 the following year, completing their withdrawal from Ditton Priors, and the base was handed over to the RAF without ceremony.

Workmen are propping up with timber the historic ruins of Lilleshall Abbey, preventing danger of collapse. The threat has come about as a result of mining operations near the abbey. The west arch is pictured, supported by beams. It is May 1961.

Mr and Mrs John Mason, of The Square, Newport, bought a piano, but then faced the problem of getting it into their flat. A giant crane provided the answer, lifted it up to the second floor, and through one of their windows while onlookers cheered. This picture was taken on February 11, 1971, and is of particular interest because it includes a rare view of Herbert Tucker's shop in the background. Tucker's shop collapsed on August 3, 1989, while being worked on, injuring three passersby. Amid various delays and wrangles over what to do in the aftermath, the site was left boarded up for so long that it became dubbed "The Shame of Newport". Eventually the district council stepped in and bought the site and it was not until 1999 that it was redeveloped with 15 homes.

Civic leaders in Oswestry had a traditional stirrup cup drink with members of the hunt in February 1971.

Flashback to June 1961, and a look at an unusual Gothic-style country cottage near Craven Arms. Predominantly 18th century, the cottage occupied a secluded woodland spot on the private estate of Major Hubert Holden, of Sibdon Castle. He offered it on a long lease to a family who would appreciate its lovely surroundings and who would be prepared to put it in good order. The family chosen were the Mount family, who began working on it to turn it into a summer and weekend retreat, a job they thought would take 10 years.

We can't imagine what the photographer was thinking of when he took this shot of Hodnet Hall in October 1967. Or maybe we can. It is a last look at the hall in its old form, as in 1967 permission was given to demolish two-thirds of Hodnet Hall because the house was "uneconomical". The hall was reshaped, essentially by removing the entire upper part.

Hodnet Hall again, or rather the side of the road leading out of Hodnet near the hall. Work is in progress on September 26, 1967, to create an unusual memorial, and one of the last great follies of that era. The pillars were put up as a memorial to Brigadier Algernon Heber-Percy of Hodnet Hall. A great lover of landscape gardening, he developed the hall gardens into a big public attraction. It was he who had acquired the portico of Apley Castle – a grand mansion near Wellington and home of the Meyrick family, who were great friends of the brigadier's – which was demolished in 1956. He planned to make the portico into a landmark feature, but died in 1961 before his dream could be realised. The project was completed by family and friends in his memory. The construction was done over nearly three weeks in September and October 1967 and two 20-ton cranes were used to haul the pillars into position. Not all the portico was put up, because it was feared to do so would make the structure unstable. The other pieces are in store.

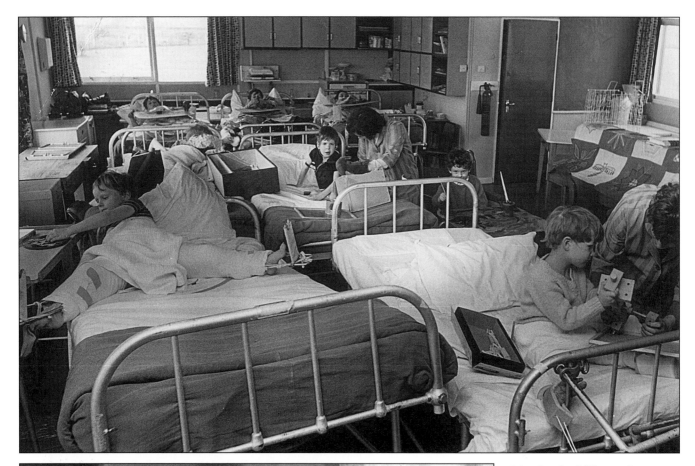

Schooling for children at the
Shropshire Orthopaedic Hospital at
Gobowen in April 1971.

A Mr Vaughan takes a peek into a
chest hewn out of a solid tree trunk
at Morville Church in January 1959.

"Thomas Telford's cast-iron aqueduct, at present on a disused part of the Shropshire Union Canal at Longdon-on-Tern, is to be moved to the Blists Hill canal, Coalport. It will become part of the Ironbridge Gorge Museum, for which a £1m appeal has just been launched," confidently asserted the story which accompanied this picture, taken on April 21, 1969. Standing on the aqueduct, from left, are: Mr E. Bruce Ball, chairman of the museum trust; Mr E.N. (Ted) Ireland, editor of the *Shropshire Star*; Mr Isaiah Jones, deputy chairman of Telford Development Corporation and a member of the trust; and Mr Emyr Thomas, general manager of the corporation and the trust's secretary. Despite what was said at the time, the aqueduct never did go to Blists Hill. It is still at Longdon-on-Tern and celebrated its bicentenary in 1996.

The village of Little Wenlock was for years blighted by mining all around. At times the village seemed to be marooned in a desert landscape. This is opencast mining on the New Works road in 1963.

Who is this young man taking a close look at the font –
believed to be early Saxon – at Shawbury church on
January 21, 1953? Cast your eye back a couple of photos
and see if you see any similarity with Mr E.N. Ireland,
the first editor of the *Shropshire Star*. Yes, this is one and
the same – Ted Ireland in his reporting days.

A hive of activity at the site of the new reservoir at Chelmarsh in December
1965.

Senior air traffic control officer at RAF Cosford, Flight Lieutenant Alex Donaldson, makes his contribution to the fuel crisis by inspecting the
airfield on horseback instead of by car. Alex was officer in charge of the Cosford Saddle Club and here combines work with pleasure. It is
November 1973.

Sort this lot out! Cross Street, Ellesmere, boasted a bewildering collection of traffic signs for the motorist back in 1966.

Now this is what you call a fire engine. It would be considered an antique by television's Fireman Sam. And it would look decidedly out of place in the gritty TV drama, *London's Burning*. But it's a good old chunky fire engine nonetheless. The picture is from February 1969 and it is of Market Drayton fire station.

Old Atcham Bridge. As a new Atcham Bridge was built alongside and opened in 1929, we can date this picture before that, perhaps to the winter of 1926-27, as work on the new bridge started in May 1927 and is not visible here. A pencil-written note on the back of the print gives some information: "Atcham Bridge, near Shrewsbury, which is in an unstable condition. Salop County Council on Sat. negatived a proposal for strengthening and widening it, and decided to build a new bridge. The old one will remain as an ancient monument." A new bridge was needed because of a great increase in traffic on Shropshire's roads in the 1920s, for which the old bridge was too narrow and too steep. Between 1925 and 1929 there was a 62 per cent increase in road traffic. The new Atcham Bridge over the River Severn was opened by the Minister of Transport, Herbert Morrison, on October 24, 1929.

This picture was taken for a shopping feature about Whitchurch, although only one of those on it was a genuine shopper. The "shoppers" are Miss Christine Dawson, aged 20, centre, and her colleague at Beryl's hair salon in Whitchurch, Sheila, right. Christine is now Mrs Christine Griffiths of Shrewsbury and thinks Sheila's maiden name was Williams and she later married Stewart Graham. The unidentified girl on the left was a genuine shopper, but Christine and Sheila were dragged from the hairdressers to pose. Incidentally Christine was Shropshire's first woman disc jockey. This picture dates from October 1968.

You'll have to be getting on a bit to remember school desks like these. We can't say for certain, of course, but we expect there will have been inkwells on the top, and perhaps names and initials carved in the wood here and there. These desks were in use in some of the classrooms at the Prince's Street School in Wellington in July 1968, although modern desks had already replaced them in some rooms. The Prince's Street School closed in 1970 and was subsequently converted into The Belfry Theatre, which officially opened on October 7, 1971, with an old time music hall in Victorian costume. It is now officially called The Belfrey Theatre after the name was misspelt on all the literature in the 1980s. It was, it seems, easier to change the name than correct all the literature!

The remains of Malinslee Chapel lie "in store" at Hinkshay, opposite the Ever Ready factory, where they are being looked over by Ever Ready employee Bill Carter on March 21, 1972. There were 400 individually numbered stones. They had been moved to the site after the Norman chapel was dismantled in, we think, April 1971, to make way for Telford town centre.

Tramps and the homeless lay mattresses in the dormitory of the casual ward at Morda House, near Oswestry, in August 1956. The closure of "Morda Vagrants' Hospital" was expected "soon", according to the caption.

A February 1939 view of the new bridge over the River Severn built near the old Highley-Alveley ferry. It was not, however, a public bridge – it was built to enable miners and coal to pass between the two villages.

This unusual signpost at Little Brampton, between Craven Arms and Clun, was ordered by the second Lord Clive, later Earl of Powis, in 1800. Since this picture was taken in August 1955 the setting of the sign has been altered by the growth of the vegetation around it.

A morning scene at Innage Lane County Infants' School, Bridgnorth, where, in March 1971, 20 children were having their lessons in a gloomy corridor a short step from the lavatories. In the afternoons the youngsters were able to move into a classroom.

The building of the Harley bypass on October 21, 1966. The old road can be seen at the bottom and the Wenlock Edge is in the distance.

The new resident, Miss Ethel Clarke, of the Staffordshire village of Marchington, watches her furniture being unloaded at Preston Hospital, which was built in the early 18th century as a home for poor women and girls. The hospital was at Preston-on-the-Weald Moors. This picture dates from October 27, 1952. Preston Trust Homes (as it was known) finally became uneconomic and had trouble attracting tenants – not everybody wants to live in the middle of nowhere, or live in a bedsit. The building was sold by the trust in 2002. Planning permission was given to turn it into eight new apartments and build five new homes at the site. A replacement building was built off Forton Road, Newport.

Jam today. A seemingly never-ending stream of traffic on the A5 at Ketley on May 30, 1966, which was obviously the Bank Holiday. Until the building of the Wellington bypass (M54) the A5 was the main route for holidaymakers on their way to the Welsh coast, with inevitably grim results.

GREEN SHIELD stamps

National

GREEN SHIELD

DOUBLE GREEN SHIELD

OPEN A

GREEN SHIELD stamps

Mrs J. Nester and Mrs H.W. Strand draw water in the cloister-like verandah at Preston Trust Homes in February 1958.

One of the biggest changes to Shropshire in recent times is down to this man, Colonel John Kenyon. He led a campaign in 1979 to change back the official title of the county from "Salop", to "Shropshire". More than 90 per cent of the organisations he contacted said they would like to see the county name go back to Shropshire, and many individuals also gave their support. He took his battle to Salop County Council, where he needed a two-thirds majority to scrap Salop and replace it with Shropshire on all official documents. Victory came in July 1980. He is seen celebrating his success with a new sign at Welshampton.

The whipping post at
Wenlock Guildhall, Much
Wenlock, in a picture from
(we think) around 1938.
The man is not identified.

SUBSCRIBERS

Mr and Mrs Barnett

Robin Patrick Minton

Mrs Julie Downing

Mrs Mary Sherwood

Carol Broadhurst

Richard David Parker

Kenneth Phillips

Mrs J Oakley

Chris and Mike Rayner

Elsie Davis

Mr Mervyn J Jewkes

Micky W Long

H J Wood

Dorothy May Harris

Robert Groves

P Ashford

Richard Bond

Tony Preece

Kenneth Hughes

Clifford Smout

Miss Gill Tunna

N R Gilmore

Patricia Jeavons

Alison Jennifer Waters

Norman Albert Rumsby

Mr L B Grandfield

Dennis and Melville Rogers

James Lloyd

Frederick Charles Williams

Veronica Ann Harrison

David John Tranter

Horace Arrowsmith

David and Betty Lake

Glyn Brace

Sandra Worrall

John Michael Smith

Pamela Living

The Oswestry Acorn Group

Miss Ann Manners

John F Marcham

Anthony J Pulford

Graham Nangreave

Anthony Harland

Trevor A W Booth-Jarvis

Doreen Evans

Stuart H Morris

John Braddick

Mrs Trixie R Fisher, BA(Hons), (nee Philpott)

Norman and Mary Lewis

Dr K B Sherwood

Mr B J Sherwood

Alan Frederick Blocksidge

Karl Dovaston, USA

Taylor Williams, Oswestry

In memory of Mrs S B Jack

Tommy Preston

Elaine Preece

Auriel Elizabeth Hayward

Mrs E. Leesley (nee Doody)

David R B Adams